D0883545

PLEASURES AND TREASURES

GRAND PRIX CHAMPIONSHIP

1950-70

ANTHONY PRITCHARD

GRAND PRIX CHAMPIONSHIP 1950-70

GROSSET & DUNLAP
A National General Company
Publishers New York

Acknowledgements

The author and publishers would like to express their gratitude to the following owners, photographers and agencies by whose permission the illustrations are reproduced: Autocar, 19, 49, 75, 91, 94b; B.P. Ltd, 66b, 83b; Bernard Cahier, 41a; Michael Cooper, 78; Daimler-Benz AG, 40a; Edward Eves, 48l; Geoffrey Goddard, frontispiece, 36b, 41b, 54 m, 64t, 85l; Guy Griffiths Motofoto, 10, 15, 17, 18a, 18b, 19, 20, 21t, 21b, 22, 23, 24–5, 31, 34, 35a, 37a, 37b, 81r, 88t, 88b, 89, 90t, 100, 105b, 108a; Behram Kapadia, 76, 92; Klemantaski Studio, 48r; T. C. March, 9, 28, 29, 30, 32, 36a, 39, 40b, 45l, 45a, 46, 47b, 51, 58, 59, 60t, 60b, 62, 65, 70, 71, 72–3t, 72–3b, 77, 79b, 81b, 83t, 85r, 98tl, 98tr, 105a, 106t, 106b; Motor, 8, 33, 54b, 56a, 90b, 95; Motor Sport, 43a, 43b, 47a, 54t, 56r, 74b, 79r, 103l; Officine Alfieri Maserati, 53; David Phipps, 64b, 67, 68, 69, 74a, 84t, 84b, 93; Anthony Pritchard Collection, 57, 66t, 82, 98lb; Publifoto, 6, 11, 35b, 52, 55; Nigel Snowdon, 86, 94a, 96–7, 99, 101, 102, 103r, 104, 107l, 1074, 108b, 109, 110a, 110b.

Frontispiece: Lodovico Scarfiotti at the wheel of his Ferrari during the 1966 Italian Grand Prix which he won.

Library of Congress Catalog No.: 75–156325
American ISBN 0-448-02588-4
Printed in Great Britain.

Contents

SUPERAGIP
IL PNEUMATICO
ELASTICO
PIRELLI
IL PNEUMATICO
ROBUSTO
PIRELLI
IL PNEUMATICO
SICURO
PIRELLI
PIRELLI

Introduction

Motor racing originated before the turn of the century, but the first Grand Prix as such was the Grand Prix de l'Automobile Club de France held in 1906. It was only after the popularity of motor racing had increased and other countries instituted their own National Grands Prix that the French race became known popularly as the French Grand Prix. The sport gradually expanded until there were each year six or eight National Grands Prix held throughout Europe and many other less important races for Grand Prix cars that took their name from the town or circuit at which they were held. Certain races became known as Grandes Épreuves which meant those races which, because of the length of time they have been established, are given priority of date in the International Calendar by the Fédération Internationale de l'Automobile, the governing body of motor sport. It was not, however, until the 1950 season that the F.I.A. introduced the Drivers' World Championship.

Until the late 1950s the principal teams competing in Grand Prix racing were all those of established motor manufacturing companies, such as Alfa Romeo, Mercedes-Benz and Lancia or racing car specialists closely associated with a large industrial concern as were Vanwall and Maserati. The Ferrari team was the only important organisation that was independent (apart from receiving a subsidy from Fiat) and yet created primarily for the purpose of motor racing. Team spirit and team co-operation were of paramount importance and all in the team were concerned that the team should score a victory rather than that the number one driver score a few more Championship points. But the immense prestige and financial benefits to be derived from a victory in the Drivers' Championship

The starting grid of the 1951 Italian Grand Prix, dominated by Alfa Romeos and Ferraris. Ascari won the race for Scuderia Ferrari.

Stirling Moss never won the Drivers' Championship, but could there have been a greater Champion?

coupled with the ever-spiralling costs of motor racing that make teams dependent financially on subsidies received from fuel and tyre companies have gradually transformed the face of Grand Prix racing.

Teams have tended to become smaller and more closely knit and it is now rare for any team to field cars for more than two drivers. During the last decade the wheel has turned full circle and several leading drivers have become constructors in their own right and drive cars bearing their own names. Two of these, Brabham and Surtees, are ex-World Champions, while other teams, notably Tyrrell, have built new cars specifically for their leading driver. So, today, Grand Prix racing is a professional and highly sophisticated sport contested between drivers rather than manufacturers and in this respect is in complete contrast with Sports Car racing where the battle is between manufacturers' teams and the drivers – many of whom also compete in Grand Prix racing – receive less publicity than the cars.

The Drivers' Championship is a very rough and ready yardstick as to driving ability, for no Champion gains this honour unless he has a car that is at least as fast and reliable as that of his rivals. The Manufacturers' Championship, introduced for the 1958 season, has received less publicity and

At Aintree in 1955 Mike Hawthorn drove this 625 Ferrari.

is surrounded by less glamour and public acclaim. With the exception of 1958, when Mike Hawthorn won the Drivers' Championship by one point from Stirling Moss and Vanwall won the Manufacturers' Championship, the latter has always been won by the team that entered the Champion driver.

When the Drivers' Championship was first held, all the rounds with one notable exception were in Europe. That exception was the Indianapolis 500 Miles race which in 1950–6 was held to the same Formula as the European races. The Indianapolis cars, however, were designed specifically for racing on a banked track and were not suitable for use in European road racing events. The only driver to compete in both before 1960, the last year in which Indianapolis counted towards the Championship, was Alberto Ascari who drove a Ferrari in the American race in 1952. As motor racing increased in popularity, so the Championship spread round the World with an Argentinian round being added in 1953, an American (a road as opposed to banked track race) in 1959, a Mexican in 1963 and a Canadian in 1967.

At the present time Grand Prix racing is one of the most popular of sports, as well as one of the most dangerous. And for the men prepared to risk its dangers and who have skill and judgment, the rewards of success are truly great.

CHAPTER ONE

Duel of the Giants, 1950-1

1950

(*Above*) Belgian driver Johnny Claes drove this yellow-painted Lago-Talbot in the 1950 European Grand Prix at Silverstone.

(*Opposite*) At the Italian Grand Prix the new 4.5-litre Ferrari appeared. Ascari's Ferrari is sandwiched between the Alfa Romeos of Farina and Fangio during the opening laps of the race.

TWENTY years ago motor racing was an awe-inspiring spectacle, an epic battle waged between beefy, muscular men – nearly all originating from the European mainland – and their vast, ponderous cars, as much as between the rival teams; and although races were shorter, cars more sophisticated and tracks smoother than in the early days of the sport, stamina and endurance were still almost as important as judgment and reaction.

Driving styles were still evolving from the brutal press-on approach that had characterised the sport since its inception before the turn of the century to a relaxed, more detached mastery of the wheel and this transition was primarily attributable to Giuseppe Farina whose vast experience extended back to pre-war days when he had driven for Scuderia Ferrari, the entrant of Alfa Romeos on behalf of the works. Farina's more inclined driving position with outstretched arms was to influence a whole generation of drivers and Stirling Moss was to prove his most inspired pupil. In 1950 Farina was again driving Alfa Romeos and his team-mates were the Argentinian Juan Fangio whose prematurely receding hair-line and gentle, experienced eyes belied his fiery determination and youthful vigour, and the veteran Italian driver Luigi Fagioli who in the early 'thirties had accomplished the difficult task of instructing other drivers on how to achieve the best from their immensely powerful 4-litre Mercedes cars.

Alfa Romeo had dominated post-war racing with their Tipo 158 straight-eight 1479 cc (58×70 mm) car that was now entering its sixth season of racing. At the end of 1948 the Milan team had withdrawn from racing as it was convinced that the 'Alfetta', first raced in 1938, was not likely to provide serious

competition for the new Ferrari and the long-awaited V-16 B.R.M. that was due to appear in 1949. But the anticipated strength of the opposition had failed to materialise in 1949 and so the 158 returned to the fray with the benefit of twelve months' development work that had boosted power output to 350 bhp at 8600 rpm. From the first race of the season it was evident that the Alfas were still the fastest cars and they completely dominated the 1950 season.

The new Tipo 125 Ferrari powered by a 60-degree V-12 engine of 1498 cc (55 × 52.5 mm) had proved very disappointing. Sponsored by the most experienced man in motor racing, Enzo Ferrari, whose connections with the sport dated back to 1919, and designed by Gioacchino Colombo who had been responsible for the Alfa Romeo 158, the Grand Prix Ferrari was deficient in both power and roadholding. The original version that had made its debut in the 1948 Italian Grand Prix had developed only 225 bhp at 7500 rpm, and, even in the absence of the Alfas, it had not performed in 1949 with particular distinction. The swing-axle independent rear suspension had provided the cars with indifferent road-holding characteristics and a notable lack of high-speed directional stability. At the 1949 European Grand Prix at Monza, Ferrari had introduced a much improved version of the Tipo 125 with gear-driven twin overhead camshafts per bank of cylinders instead of the original chain-driven single cam layout and to improve roadholding the chassis was lengthened and widened. These supercharged cars were raced by Ferrari until a new unsupercharged design gradually replaced them as the season progressed. Ferrari's drivers were Alberto Ascari, son of the great Antonio Ascari who had lost his life in the 1925 French Grand Prix and Luigi Villoresi, a very experienced driver who had handled Maseratis in pre-war days. Ferrari also had the services of Dorino Serafini, yet another Italian, and English privateer Peter Whitehead raced his own Ferrari with assistance from the works.

As for the opposition, it was almost non-existent. Another Italian contender, the Maserati 4CLT/48 'San Remo' had not been developed further since its appearance two years previously and, in any case, this Modena concern did not field its own team, but left the marque's representation entirely in the hands of private owners. The blue of France was represented by the 4482 cc (93 × 110 mm) 6-cylinder unsupercharged

Talbots that thundered round the circuits ponderously and majestically, without any real turn of speed. The other French contender was the diminutive Simca, financed by the car manufacturing company of that name and designed by Amédée Gordini. These cars were too under-powered and too unreliable to achieve any success. Wearing the British Racing Green were the E.R.A.s; in the main these were pre-war cars and their day was long passed even though Bob Gerard had performed miracles by driving these cars into third place in the 1948 British Grand Prix and into second place in the following year's race. In addition there were the two E-type cars built in 1939 as successors to the original models. Although these were extensively developed in post-war days and were not lacking in potential, their early promise was never fulfilled and in the whole of their career – 1950 was their last year – they failed to win a single race.

The first round in the Championship was the European Grand Prix held at the bleak, characterless Silverstone former airfield circuit in Northamptonshire. The course was lined at the corners by straw bales and its flatness and lack of atmosphere was in sharp contrast with the true road circuits used for the Continental rounds in the Championship. Alfa Romeo fielded four cars, three for the three 'F's and the fourth, which would have been entrusted to the team's head tester and chief mechanic Consalvo Sanesi, but for injuries he had sustained in a crash in the Mille Miglia sports car race, was handled by Reg Parnell; this was the only occasion on which a British driver appeared at the wheel of a 158.

Ferrari did not run in the race and the four Alfas cantered to victory. Fagioli, his bulky figure looking cramped in the cockpit and leaning forward as he changed gear, led initially, but then Farina went ahead. After his refuelling stop, Fangio moved up into second place. Five laps from the finish, the Argentinian's car retired with a broken connecting rod and Fagioli moved up into second place, finishing three seconds behind the winner. Parnell, the only member of the team to wear a crash helmet instead of the traditional linen helmet, took third place, the front of his car dented and gashed in a collision with a hare.

In the Monaco Grand Prix, what had prospects of being a great race evaporated on the first lap when Giuseppe Farina, in second place, spun on a pool of water, hit a wall and bounced off into the path of a Maserati. In the multi-car pile-up that this triggered off, eight cars were eliminated and when Fangio, leading the race, reached the scene of the accident on his second lap, he found that the road was blocked. He was indicated the wrong way round the crashed cars by the marshalls and heaving on the enormous 18-inch wheels of his Alfa, he succeeded in rolling the car backwards and was then able to manoeuver round the accident. Fangio was now completely unopposed and with the cars of team-mates Farina and Fagioli out of the race he scored an easy victory from Ascari's Ferrari.

In June was the Swiss Grand Prix held on the Bremgarten circuit near Berne which was set in wooded countryside and very difficult to drive on in strong sunshine because of the play of shadow from the trees across the road surface. Facing the three Alfas of Farina, Fangio and Fagioli were the Ferraris of Ascari and Villoresi. Villoresi drove the latest car from the 'Prancing Horse' stable with shortened chassis, de Dion axle and 4-speed gearbox, while Ascari had one of the usual cars. In the opening laps Ascari forced his Ferrari between the leading Alfas of Farina and Fagioli, but both of the V-12 cars were the early victims of mechanical troubles. Fangio retired with valve trouble in the closing stages of the race.

At the Maranello works of Ferrari a new designer had replaced Colombo; the design of a new Grand Prix car had been the most important task facing tubby, genial Aurelio Lampredi and the first fruits of his work had been seen in the Mille Miglia where Ascari and Villoresi drove new 3.3-litre cars, the engines of which were intended for use in Grand Prix racing. The Ferrari team had decided that the day of the supercharged engine with its high internal stresses and phenomenal thirst for fuel were over and had embarked on the development of an unsupercharged Grand Prix car, still of V-12 layout and incorporating most of the basic features of the original Colombo design. The first of these cars, with the interim 3322 cc engine mounted in the usual long wheelbase chassis, was driven by Ascari in the Belgian Grand Prix on the very fast Spa circuit. Villoresi had a normal supercharged car. Once again the race was an Alfa Romeo benefit, but French driver Raymond Sommer with a Lago-Talbot succeeded in taking the lead while the Italian cars stopped to refuel. Sad to relate, the over-driven Talbot blew up its engine and the Alfas

What should have been a day of glory for Britain – the 1950 *Daily Express* Trophy at Silverstone. B.R.M. chief Raymond Mays talks to driver Raymond Sommer who was at the wheel of the new V-16 car on its race debut. The B.R.M. failed to leave the start-line because of transmission failure.

of Fangio and Fagioli took the first two places. Farina's Alfa was slowed by gearbox trouble and finished fourth behind Louis Rosier's Talbot. It was not a happy race for Ferrari, as the best his drivers could manage was fifth and sixth places, with Ascari leading from his team-mate.

At the beginning of July was the French Grand Prix and although the unsupercharged Ferrari appeared in practice, the entry was scratched. Yet again Alfa Romeo completely dominated the results on this fast road circuit on the outskirts of the famous cathedral city of Reims; Fangio and Fagioli took the first two places, while Farina was eliminated by fuel pump trouble.

One more round in the Championship was still to be held, the Italian race in September, but before then a number of interesting developments were to be seen at less important races. In the Grand Prix des Nations at Geneva on 30 July, Ferrari revealed his latest 4101 cc unsupercharged car and this was driven by Ascari, while Villoresi had the 3.3-litre version. When holding fifth place, Villoresi crashed badly, but Ascari chased the Alfas hard and was in second place when he retired the Ferrari with water pouring out of the exhausts. The Alfas also ran in the *Daily Express* Trophy race at Silverstone on 26 August, but the sensation of the meeting was to be the new V-16 B.R.M., Britain's great racing hope initiated by Raymond Mays and financed and assisted by hundreds of companies associated with the motor industry. After grave doubts as to whether the very complex B.R.M. would reach the starting line because of persistent engine trouble during testing, the car appeared with the great French driver Raymond Sommer at the wheel. When the Union Jack fell for the start of the race, the sleek, pale green car gave a violent shudder and stayed where it was as the rest of the field disappeared into the distance in a cloud of rubber smoke. The trouble was drive-shaft failure. Although the B.R.M. was raced again at the end of the following month, the V-16 cars never achieved substantial success and it is only in recent years that the team, now a member of the Rubery Owen industrial complex, has succeeded in shedding memories of the disgrace and ignominy that cloaked its early efforts.

Before the Italian race held at Monza, Juan Fangio led the World Championship with 26 points to Fagioli's 24 and Farina's 22. For this race both Fangio and Farina were given the latest Tipo 159 cars that were 20 bhp more powerful, while Fagioli, Sanesi and Piero Taruffi drove the older versions. From Ferrari came the latest development of his unsupercharged theme, the full 4498 cc (80 × 74.5 mm) version developing 330 bhp at 7000 rpm. Ascari made an excellent start with his new Ferrari and battled with the Alfas for the lead until his engine blew up. Fangio's Alfa retired with a seized gearbox, and both victory in the race and the World Championship went to Nino Farina. After the retirement of his own car, Ascari took over that of team-mate Dorino Serafini and brought it through the field to finish second ahead of Fagioli's Alfa. The race had revealed that the unblown Ferraris were rapidly becoming a serious threat to Alfa supremacy and the following month – albeit in the absence of Alfa opposition – Ascari, Serafini and Taruffi took the first three places in the non-Championship Penya Rhin Grand Prix through the streets of Barcelona.

1951

For the coming season Alfa Romeo concentrated their efforts on increasing power output and in bench tests the power units of the 1951 version of the Tipo 159 were attaining 405 bhp at

(*Opposite*) 1950 World Champion Giuseppe Farina at the wheel of his 158 Alfa Romeo in the British Grand Prix. He won the race at 90.95 mph.

(*Above*) Juan Fangio, World Champion-to-be, flinging his 159 Alfa Romeo round Silverstone in pursuit of the leading Ferrari. (*Below*) Winner of the Silverstone race was Froilan Gonzalez (Ferrari).

10,500 rpm. In the interests of reliability, however, drivers usually restricted their engine speed to 8500 rpm. So much of the Alfa's fuel was now being used for internal cooling that the cars were consuming methanol at the rate of 1.6 mpg and in all the longer races two refuelling stops were needed with the normal fuel capacity. So additional tanks were mounted around the cockpit and, sometimes, alongside the engine. The additional weight affected roadholding and to combat this problem the Alfa engineers, who were once again headed by Colombo, the car's original designer, evolved a simple de Dion rear axle which was used in some races. Fagioli had been dropped from the Alfa Romeo team and his place was taken by another Italian driver, Felice Bonetto, who had previously driven Maseratis. At the beginning of the season the Ferraris were unchanged apart from the introduction of twin-plug ignition which boosted power output to 380 bhp at 7000 rpm and improved brakes.

Because the British race had been postponed until later in the year, the first round in the 1951 Championship was the Swiss Grand Prix. This race was run in torrential rain throughout and Fangio drove magnificently to victory but Farina lost second place to Piero Taruffi's Ferrari.

At the Belgian race only thirteen starters appeared on the grid; there were only three makes of car present – Alfa Romeo, Ferrari and Lago-Talbot. Of these, only the Lago-Talbots ran through the race without refuelling. The early laps saw the Alfa Romeos and Ferraris scrapping furiously, but then Farina and Fangio pulled clearly ahead of the Maranello opposition. When Farina stopped to refuel, he lost the lead to Fangio, but then it was Fangio's turn to stop for fuel and new tyres. When the mechanics tried to remove the left-hand rear wheel, it was found that a spoke-head had forced its way behind the hub splines. After the mechanics had struggled in vain with the wheel, it proved necessary to remove the tyre from the rim and when a frustrated Fangio rejoined the race after fifteen minutes' delay, he had lost all chance of doing well. At the chequered flag, Farina was just under three minutes ahead of Ascari's Ferrari, Villoresi was third, a full lap ahead of Louis Rosier's Talbot, and the unlucky Fangio finished ninth and last, but with the meagre consolation of having set fastest lap of the race at 120.51 mph in his efforts to make up lost time.

Grand Prix racing was now in the throes of an epic struggle between two strong teams: Alfa Romeo straining to maintain their superiority and Ferrari within a hair's breadth of snatching it from them. In the European Grand Prix at Reims the struggle continued, but the fight between the Italian teams devolved into a succession of mechanical failures and driver swaps. At the chequered flag Fangio was a minute ahead of Ascari who had taken over Gonzalez' car.

The British race witnessed a fantastic duel between Fangio and fellow-Argentinian Gonzalez with a works, but 1950 single-plug Ferrari and despite all Fangio's screaming revs and forceful cornering, the tables were turned, Gonzalez forged ahead when Fangio stopped to refuel and scored a brilliant victory. The scene then switched to the Nürburgring. The race, the German Grand Prix, was of significance for two reasons. Firstly, because it was the first Formula One race to be held in Germany since the war and secondly because the eyes of the whole motor racing world were focused on the circuit to see whether the now highly developed Ferraris could maintain the brilliant form shown at Silverstone.

(*Above*) In the 1951 Silverstone race the two B.R.M.s were among the finishers but both drivers, Parnell and Walker, were badly burnt by overheating cockpits.

(*Overleaf*) (*Left*) A cockpit view of the 4.5-litre Ferrari showing the simple instrumentation. (*Right, top*) For the 1953 season Belgian driver Johnny Claes bought this Connaught from the works. The car is seen at Silverstone. (*Bottom*) French Champion Louis Rosier with his Ferrari Tipo 500 in 1953.

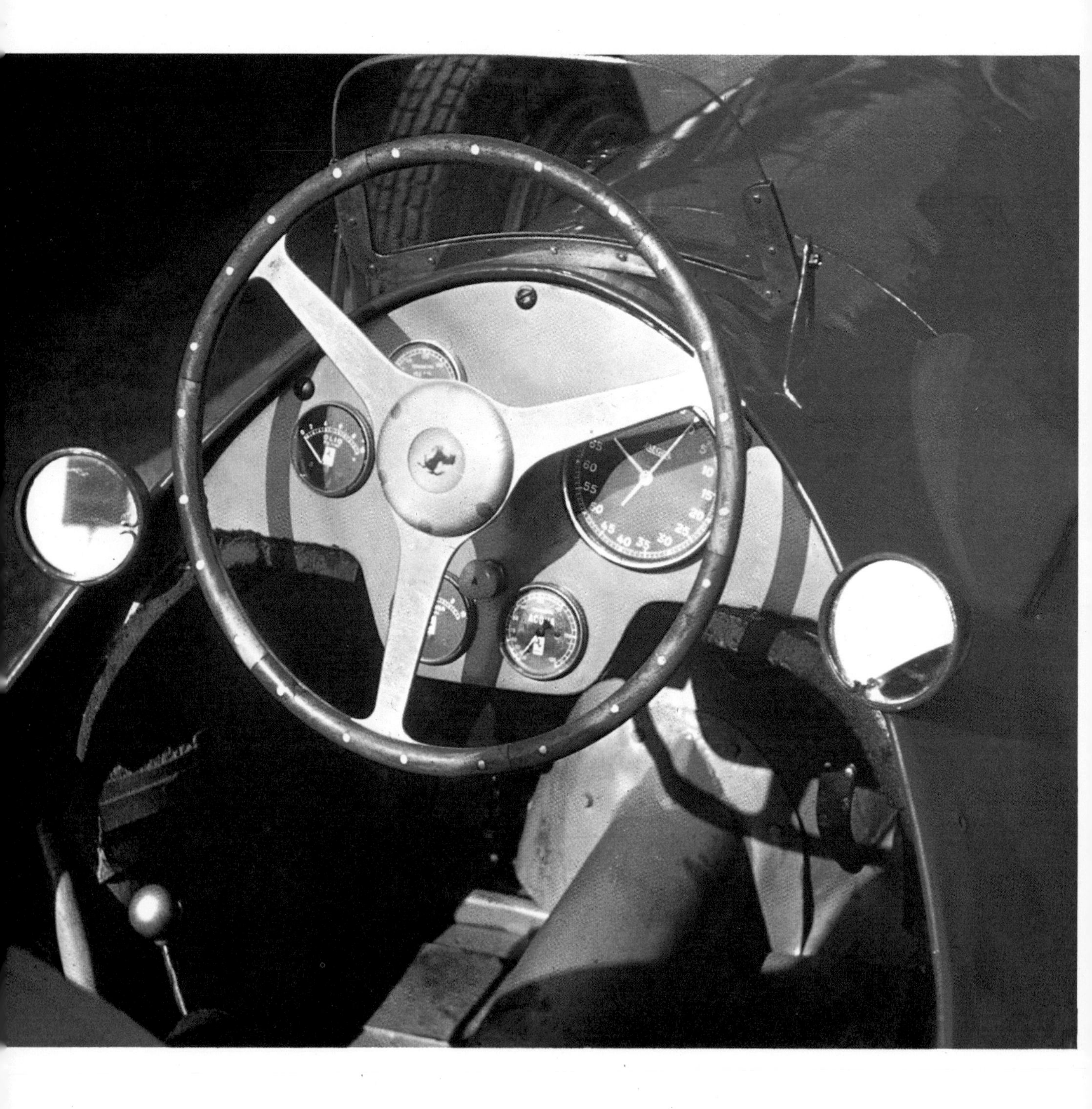
OLIO
ACQUA

19

15

(*Above*) The potent-looking V-12 power unit of the Osca; here it is seen in 1951 as originally installed in a Maserati chassis.

In this race both Fangio and Farina drove Alfas fitted with de Dion rear axles and German driver Paul Pietsch was included in the team. After one lap Fangio's Alfa led from the Ferraris of Ascari and Gonzalez and these three cars soon outpaced the rest of the field. Ascari took the lead on lap four and as the Alfas needed to refuel twice and the Ferraris only once, it already looked as though the race would provide another Ferrari victory. Nor were the Alfas blessed by good fortune, for Farina was eliminated by gearbox trouble and supercharger failure eliminated Bonetto's car. When Paul Pietsch spun his Alfa off the track, the only Milan car left in the race was that of Fangio. The Argentinian was in a fighting mood and re-took the lead from Ascari, but he was unable to gain sufficient time to compensate for the valuable seconds lost in his second refuelling stop. Although Ascari made an unscheduled stop for new rear tyres in the closing stages of the race, he did not lose his lead and Fangio finished second, almost thirty seconds in arrears.

The Ferraris had defeated the Alfas on a medium-speed circuit (Silverstone) and a slow, difficult road circuit (the Nürburgring) and it now remained to be seen whether they could match the sheer speed of the Milan cars on the very fast Monza course. Before the Italian race there was the Bari Grand Prix, a minor race which both Alfa Romeo and Ferrari entered. Although Farina (Alfa) and Ascari and Villoresi (Ferraris) all retired, the surviving 159 of Fangio soundly trounced the Maranello entry of Gonzalez. It seemed that perhaps Alfa had stemmed the flood of defeats and the odds on an Alfa victory rose even higher when the team revealed at the Italian race an improved model known as the 159M (*Maggiorata*). These cars, with stiffened chassis, de Dion axles as standard, slight engine modifications and longer tails, were driven by Fangio, Farina and Bonetto, while Emmanuel de Graffenried, a Swiss ace deputising for Sanesi who had been badly burnt during refuelling practice, had a normal 159 car. Ferrari entered a grand total of five cars and those driven by Ascari, Villoresi and Gonzalez were distinguished by new and higher tails.

On the very first lap the Alfa of de Graffenried retired with a seized supercharger. After only three laps Farina's car retired with lubrication trouble and he was obliged to wait until Bonetto stopped to refuel on lap 29 before he could take over his car. Ascari and Fangio were battling for the lead, but on lap 13 the Alfa threw a front tyre tread and Fangio was forced to stop for a wheel-change with the result that he dropped back to fifth place. The Argentinian was far from beaten and with his Alfa screaming at full pitch, he had regained second place behind Ascari by lap 30. Alfa efforts were, however, doomed that day and when Fangio retired with engine failure on lap 38, Ascari's victory was assured. Farina had succeeded in getting back on to the same lap as the two leading Ferraris, but a fuel leak necessitated an unscheduled stop, and he finished third, having set a new lap record of 120.97 mph.

In three successive Championship races Ferrari had defeated the thirteen-year-old Alfa Romeos and vindicated his policy of building unsupercharged cars. Before the season ended, there was one more Championship race, the Spanish Grand Prix, and a quirk of fate was to twist the tail of Ferrari's prancing horse and ensure that the Alfetta's career ended on a happy note. At Barcelona the Ferrari team ran on 16-inch rear wheels, whereas the Alfas were on 18-inch rear wheels. The high speeds attained along the circuit's bumpy straight, the Avenida Generalísimo Franco, set up unexpected strains on the large-section, but comparatively small-diameter tyres. The result was that the Ferraris were plagued by constant tyre trouble and Taruffi retired when his car lost a wheel. So Juan Fangio at the wheel of a 159 won the race and clinched his victory in the Drivers' Championship.

This Grand Prix Formula was scheduled to run until the end of the 1953 season. Alfa Romeo, however, were reluctantly forced to withdraw from racing, for the government subsidy which the team sought in order to finance a redesigned, lighter and much more powerful version of the Alfetta was not forthcoming. Racing was, therefore, in grave danger of becoming a complete Ferrari benefit. The only possible opponent for the Maranello team was the B.R.M. The result was the adoption of Formula Two for the Championship races of 1952–3.

(*Above*) A relaxed Juan Fangio seen with John Cooper of Cooper Car fame at Goodwood in 1952.

(*Overleaf*) The 4.5-litre Ferrari defeated the previously all-conquering Alfa Romeos three times during the 1951 season. This is Gonzalez' winning car in the British race.

CHAPTER TWO

Formula Two Grand Prix Racing, 1952-3

1952

FORMULA TWO, or Formula B as it was originally known, was introduced as a subsidiary and less expensive class of single-seater racing for the 1948 season. Right from its inception it had been well supported by Italian, British, French and German constructors and when the Formula was adopted for World Championship races, there was a grand total of six manufacturers regularly fielding competitive cars, two Italian, three British and one French.

Ever since the Formula had been introduced the majority of successes had fallen to the Ferrari team. The earliest Formula Two Ferraris, raced in 1948, had been V-12 cars with an engine similar in design to that of the Grand Prix cars and a chassis derived from the team's sports car practice; for the following season the Grand Prix chassis was adopted and during 1950–1 the team continued to race cars with the same engine, but with a chassis designed specifically for Formula Two use. At the Modena Grand Prix in 1951, however, there had appeared a completely new 4-cylinder 1980 cc (90 × 78 mm) car designed by Aurelio Lampredi. The power output of 170 bhp at 7000 rpm in 1952 form made the Ferrari one of the fastest cars of its class, and it combined a modest weight (1340 lb) with excellent handling, largely attributable to the well-designed de Dion rear axle in unit with which was a 4-speed gearbox. In addition to Ascari and Villoresi, the retirement of Alfa Romeo from racing made available the services of Farina, whom Ferrari quickly snapped up, and Piero Taruffi also joined the team to make a most formidable quartet. Several of the cars were also sold to private owners.

The most serious opponent for Ferrari in 1952 should have been the strong combination of Juan Fangio and the new

(*Opposite*) Brilliant climax to an exciting season came in the Italian Grand Prix where the leaders closely slip-streamed each other throughout the 312 miles. Here Fangio (Maserati) leads Farina (Ferrari) and Marimon (Maserati).

(*Overleaf*) (*Left*) Karl Kling's streamlined Mercedes-Benz W.196 in the 1954 British Grand Prix. (*Right*) Maurice Trintignant driving a Tipo 801 version of the Lancia car modified by Ferrari in the 1957 European Grand Prix at Aintree.

50

2

Maserati A6GCM. Incorporating a number of established Maserati design features, this 6-cylinder car had a capacity of 1960 cc (75 × 75 mm) and developed 165 bhp – quite adequate for the car to be competitive. The chassis was a simple and rather uninspired design with a rigid rear axle and the 4-speed gearbox was in unit with the engine. Although the new cars appeared at the Argentine 'Temporada' races at the beginning of the year, they failed to impress. Their European debut came in the non-Championship Autodrome Grand Prix at Monza, and here an exhausted Fangio, having driven across Europe after competing with a B.R.M. in the Ulster Trophy, crashed on the second lap, breaking his neck and putting himself out of racing for the rest of the season. So it was not until the Italian Grand Prix, where a new twin-plug version of the A6GCM appeared that the car made its mark.

France was represented by the new 1960 cc (75 × 75 mm) Gordini designed, built and financed (with help from friends) by Amédée Gordini in his own small workshops. Like the Maserati, the chassis design was simple and unsophisticated, but there was a 5-speed synchromesh gearbox, and the power output was 160 bhp which gave the Gordini an excellent turn of speed, and its performance was tempered only by the team's lack of financial resources and an unexpected number of mechanical failures. Gordini's drivers were Robert Manzon, who had driven Gordini's Simca cars for many years, and French motor-cycle champion Jean Behra, one of the most courageous and persevering of drivers. Yet another 6-cylinder Formula Two car was the Osca, with 1986 cc (76 × 73 mm)

Fast but fragile – the French-built Gordini. Belgian Johnny Claes drives his private 1.5-litre car in the 1952 British Grand Prix.

twin overhead camshaft engine, and built by the Maserati brothers, who had sold out their interest in the company bearing their name some years previously.

Pioneer of British Formula Two cars was the H.W.M., the brainchild of John Heath. Using the 1960 cc (79 × 100 mm) 4-cylinder twin overhead camshaft Alta engine, Heath had built in 1949 the H.W.-Alta, which could be adapted for single-seater or sports car racing. Stirling Moss was in the team during 1950–1, but left to drive in 1952 the new E.R.A. Formula Two car powered by a Bristol engine. Nevertheless the team retained Peter Collins and signed up Lance Macklin. By 1952, however, the H.W.M.s were pitifully underpowered compared with their Continental rivals.

A completely new British project for 1952 was the Cooper-Bristol built by the small firm who had achieved fame through 500 cc Formula Three racing cars. The 500 cc cars were rear-engined, but the new car had the engine mounted conventionally at the front, and this was the 6-cylinder Bristol push-rod ohv unit developed from the pre-war B.M.W. engine and powering a whole series of British competition sports cars as well as production Bristol cars. Although the Bristol engine could not be induced to develop more than 150 bhp without losing its reliability, this was compensated for by the very low weight of the Cooper chassis and the excellent roadholding provided by the independent wishbone suspension front and rear. The new car made its debut at the Easter Goodwood meeting and, after Hawthorn with his new acquisition had won two of the day's races and finished second to Gonzalez

(*Below*) Two unsuccessful British Formula Two projects – the G-type E.R.A. driven by Stirling Moss and the Alta with Graham Whitehead at the wheel.

CASTROL

with the 4.5-litre Ferrari 'Thin Wall' Special in another, both car and driver were headline news.

At Send, in Surrey, the Connaught concern were developing their own very sophisticated car which had first appeared towards the end of 1950. Although the car was handicapped by the low output of its push-rod engine developed from the production Lea-Francis unit, the chassis was probably the best thought-out of all Formula Two designs and superbly executed. In 1952 the make made few appearances in major events. Other British products worthy of mention are the Alta, and the single-seater version of the Frazer Nash sports car, also powered by the Bristol engine. Germany was represented in Formula Two racing by the Veritas, another car powered by a derivative of the B.M.W. engine, but in this case redesigned so that valve actuation was by a single overhead camshaft, and the A.F.M., designed and built by B.M.W. development engineer Alex von Falkenhausen. Neither of these makes, however, achieved an important success outside Germany.

As in 1951, the first round in the Championship was the Swiss race at Bremgarten, and although the Ferraris of Piero Taruffi and private local driver Rudi Fischer took the first two places, two of the works Maranello entries were eliminated. Farina retired his own car with magneto trouble and then took over that of André Simon only to be eliminated by exactly the same fault. Third place went to Jean Behra at the wheel of a brand-new Gordini.

In 1952 the Monaco Grand Prix was held as a sports car race and so the next race in the Championship was the European Grand Prix at Spa. In this race, held on a track soaked by torrential rain, the lower-powered cars were at less of a disadvantage on this fast circuit than would have been the case in dry conditions; although the Ferraris of Ascari and Farina took the first two places, Manzon's Gordini was third and, notwithstanding two unscheduled stops to top up the fuel tank because of a leak, young Mike Hawthorn took a brilliant fourth place – brilliant because it was both his first season of Grand Prix racing and the highest place ever achieved by a British car in a World Championship race.

Only a week later was the non-Championship Reims Grand Prix and here Jean Behra led the Ferraris throughout to score an exciting and unexpected victory for the Gordini team. Alas, Behra was unable to repeat this form the following weekend in

(*Above*) Fourth place in the 1952 Belgian Grand Prix went to the brilliant combination of young Mike Hawthorn and his Cooper Bristol.

(*Opposite*) In practice for the 1957 Aintree race is five times World Champion Juan Fangio with his Maserati 250F.

the French Grand Prix and finished a poor seventh, but other Gordinis driven by Robert Manzon and Maurice Trintignant were fourth and fifth behind the Ferrari procession. In the British race it was the Connaughts, making one of their only two Championship race appearances of the year, and Hawthorn's Cooper, that gave the Ferraris trouble. After Farina's pit stop, Ascari and Taruffi took the first two places, but Dennis Poore with his Connaught had led Taruffi in the early stages of the race and only lost third place to Hawthorn through an agonisingly slow refuelling stop. Eric Thompson finished fifth with another Connaught and it was the first time that either driver had appeared in a Championship race.

The Maranello monoply continued at the Nürburgring. Here, Ascari stopped for extra oil before starting on his last lap, Farina went into the lead, and it was only by driving right on the limit that Ascari snatched victory from the grasp of his team-mate. A new addition to the Championship was the Dutch Grand Prix, held at Zandvoort, a circuit set in the sand dunes of the North sea coast of Holland. Although Hawthorn succeeded in recording third fastest practice time and started from the front row of the grid, he was unable to overcome the power deficiency of his Cooper and finished fourth behind the three leading Ferraris. Even before the Italian Grand Prix, Ascari had amassed sufficient points to be unassailable in the World Championship, but the Monza race was one of the few that year in which his supremacy was seriously challenged. Apart from a team of Connaughts, the new twin-plug Maserati

Too late to achieve substantial success – the 4.5-litre Osca which did not find form before the then Formula One came to an end. The Siamese driver Bira is seen at Silverstone in 1952.

appeared on the scene in the hands of Froilan Gonzalez. The ponderous, surly-looking Argentinian led for 36 of the 80 laps, drawing out a lead from Ascari at the rate of a second a lap, but because of the small fuel tank of the Maserati he was forced to make a pit stop. The time lost was too great for him to be able to make up and he finished second.

1953

Despite the powerful challenge from Maserati at the end of the season, Ferrari contented himself with only minor modifications to the very successful Tipo 500 cars and power output rose to 190 bhp at 7500 rpm. On the strength of his fine performances with his Cooper-Bristol in 1952, Mike Hawthorn was invited to join the team, and he replaced Taruffi. At Modena much more intensive development work took place and the 1953 version of the Maserati was the Tipo A6SSG with revised cylinder dimensions of 76.2 × 72 mm, a power output of 190 bhp at 8000 rpm and rather more aerodynamic bodywork. Fangio was now back in racing and led a very competitive team that included Gonzalez, Bonetto and Argentinian newcomer Onofre Marimon. The new cars were not, however, ready at the beginning of the season and in the Argentinian Grand Prix in January, a new round in the Championship, the team relied on the 1952 cars. The French Gordinis were unchanged; Cooper had a new tubular chassis, but, with the loss of Hawthorn, they had no competitive driver to handle their cars; the ever-improving Connaught team was now using Hilborn-Travers fuel-injection and oxygen-bearing nitromethane fuel. The H.W.M.s were now outclassed, but the team still persevered and the 1953 cars had a Jaguar C-type synchromesh gearbox in place of the previous pre-selector box. After a wasted season in 1952 with the unsuccessful E.R.A., Stirling Moss commissioned for 1953 a very special Cooper with an Alta engine and de Dion rear axle. This car proved to be another complete failure and in mid-season the engine was transferred to a standard Cooper chassis.

In the Argentine the Ferraris took the first two places ahead of Gonzalez' Maserati and young Hawthorn proved his worth by a smooth, unspectacular drive into fourth place. The Dutch and Swiss rounds of the Championship had swapped dates in the calendar and at this first European round at Zandvoort

Unchallenged Champion – Alberto Ascari won every Championship race but the Swiss in 1952. Here he is seen on his way to victory in the British Grand Prix in his 2-litre Ferrari.

(*Below*) First serious opposition to Ferrari in 1952 came in the Italian Grand Prix where Gonzalez drove the new twin-plug Maserati into second place.

(*Above*) The dark blue and white of Rob Walker, seen in 1953 on his 2-litre Connaught driven here by Le Mans winner Tony Rolt.

(*Below*) Alberto Ascari repeated his Championship victory in 1953, still driving a 4-cylinder Ferrari. He is seen here leading the field at Silverstone.

the new Maseratis were out in force. They were, however, still too new and unsorted to challenge the Ferraris, but Gonzalez drove an inspired race, taking third place. A fortnight later the Belgian Grand Prix was held, and on the high-speed Spa circuit the Maseratis went magnificently; Gonzalez and Fangio steadily drew away from the howling pack of Maranello cars and just when it seemed that Maranello supremacy was to be crushed, the Modena challenge failed. Gonzalez and Fangio both retired with engine trouble, leaving the Ferraris in the first two places as usual.

So close, so exciting was the French Grand Prix at Reims, that one leading journalist described it as 'the race of the age'. Gonzalez started the race with a half-full tank, thereby reducing the weight of his car, and with instructions to go as fast as possible as long as possible to break up the opposition. This he did, and when he stopped to refuel he was leading from Fangio, Hawthorn and Ascari. For the rest of the race a tightly packed bunch of red cars battled furiously, slip-streaming each other closely, but always with Fangio's Maserati just in front. Then two laps from the finish the Maserati of Fangio and the Ferrari of Hawthorn crossed the finishing line side-by-side; on the next lap Hawthorn was clearly ahead, and after 312 miles of high-speed, closely-fought motor-racing he took the chequered flag a bare second ahead of Fangio. For Hawthorn this was a magnificent triumph, gained against the strongest possible opposition.

In the British race Hawthorn was decidedly off form and never in the picture, and although the Maseratis of Fangio and Gonzalez chased Ascari hard, they were not able to catch the World Champion on the deceptively difficult Silverstone circuit. It was much the same story at the Nürburgring, where Ascari was clearly master of the opposition, but on this especially ardous circuit, good fortune was not on his side. Ascari led from Fangio in the early stages of the race, but then his car lost a front wheel and he motored back to the pits on three wheels and a brake drum. A new wheel was fitted, Ascari rejoined the race in fifth place, albeit well behind the leading trio of Farina, Fangio and Hawthorn, but then swapped cars with team-mate Villoresi, who was in fourth place. Hawthorn's car was in the World Champion's sights when the engine of his Ferrari blew up and the Italian, having fought harder than at any time in his career, was forced to retire.

At Bremgarten in the Swiss race Fangio took the lead at the start, but it was not destined that there should be a Maserati victory that day and the Argentinian was forced to stop with engine trouble. Although he rejoined the race at the wheel of Bonetto's car his engine blew up and once again the Ferraris dominated the results. The teams next met at the Italian Grand Prix. At this race Ferrari fielded two new cars, the Tipo 553 'Squalo' (Shark) cars that were prototypes for the 1954 season; none of Ferrari's usual drivers was enamoured of their handling characteristics, so for the race they were given to 'cadet' drivers Umberto Maglioli and Piero Carini and neither featured high in the results. The race proved a repetition of Reims, with the Ferraris of Ascari and Farina and the Maserati of Fangio slip-streaming each other closely, swapping the lead constantly and with never as much as two seconds separating them. In the closing laps of the race this trio was joined by Marimon, who was many laps behind after two pit stops. As the cars entered the last lap Fangio, in third place, appeared to have lost all chance of winning. Then, at the last corner, Ascari's Ferrari spun viciously, Farina dived to the outside and on to the grass to avoid him and was struggling to regain control, Marimon's Maserati slammed into the spinning Ferrari, while Fangio sneaked by on the inside to take the lead and Maserati's one and only victory of the 2-litre Formula.

(*Above*) Roberto Manzon (Gordini) leads Froilan Gonzalez (Maserati) through a corner in the 1953 British Grand Prix.

(*Below*) Alberto Ascari, 1953 World Champion and one of the greatest of all Italian drivers.

CHAPTER THREE

A Golden Age of Racing, 1954-60

1954

FERRARI was ready at the beginning of the year with his Tipo 625 car which had already raced on odd occasions since 1951. This was simply the existing Tipo 500 chassis with an enlarged 2490 cc engine developing 230 bhp at 7000 rpm. By the start of the European season Ferrari also had ready to race the full 2498 cc version of the 553 'Squalo' cars that had appeared at Monza the previous year. These were a re-work of the 625 with multi-tubular space-frame, a shorter stroke, much higher revving engine and squat bodywork with pannier side-tanks. Ascari and Villoresi had left the team to drive the new Lancia when it should be ready and Farina and Hawthorn were joined by Gonzalez and, after the Argentinian races, by the Frenchman Maurice Trintignant.

Maserati, too, had contented themselves with modifying the existing cars, but the modifications were extensive. Apart from increasing engine capacity to 2493 cc (84 × 72 mm) and power output to 240 bhp, the rear suspension now incorporated a de Dion rear axle and the 4-speed gearbox was in unit with the final drive. The 250F was generally considered to be one of the prettiest cars ever raced. At the beginning of the year there was a shortage of 250F chassis and both the works and private owners raced the old A6SSG chassis with the new engine. Maserati had a steady production line of 250Fs at Modena and in due course cars were sold to private owners Prince Bira, Stirling Moss, the Owen Organisation, for Ken Wharton to drive while work progressed on the new B.R.M., and Gilby Engineering whose car was driven by Roy Salvadori. In contrast with the Italian efforts, Gordini simply contented himself with increasing the capacity of his cars to 2473 cc, but this was for reasons of economy rather than for lack of technical

The Mercedes cars of Moss and Fangio during the 1955 British Grand Prix at Aintree.

CASTROL
12
10
10

(*Above*) Brilliant race debut for the streamlined Mercedes-Benz W.196 cars at the 1954 French Grand Prix. Here Karl Kling leads by a nose from the eventual winner, Juan Fangio.

(*Below*) Battered, slowed by transmission trouble and plagued by an oil leak, Fangio's Mercedes finished a poor fourth in the 1954 British race.

inspiration and a new model followed in due course.

The Argentinian race proved a most unsatisfactory affair, for on the dry roads on which the early stages of the race were run, Fangio's Maserati was no match for the works Ferraris; then the circuit was enveloped in a sudden rain-squall; Fangio went ahead, the rain ceased, and the Ferraris of Gonzalez and Farina both repassed him. When the rain started to fall again Fangio came into the pits for his car to be fitted with a special set of rain tyres cut as the race proceeded. No sooner had the Maserati left the pits than the Ferrari team manager Ugolini protested that more than the permitted number of mechanics had worked on the Ferrari. On the assumption that his protest would be upheld he slowed his cars down, and Fangio repassed them without difficulty. To Ferrari's dismay, the protest was rejected, and Fangio won the race. The Belgian race was much more clear-cut. Fangio took the lead on lap 3 and led for the remainder of the race except for three laps when Farina went ahead with his 'Squalo' only to retire with ignition trouble.

Fangio's contract with Maserati provided that he would only drive the Modena cars until the new Mercedes was raceworthy, and he appeared at the wheel of the new car at Reims, the third round in the Championship. Mercedes, whose technical resources were second to none, had the advantage of starting with a clean drawing board and no pre-conceived

ideas. Their new W.196 car was both revolutionary and excessively complex. The power unit was a straight-eight 2496 cc (76 × 68.8 mm) design of very advanced thinking in that it had both fuel injection and desmodromic valves (without valve springs) laid almost horizontal in the chassis to achieve a very small frontal area. This advanced unit developed 270 bhp at 8200 rpm and was substantially more powerful than any of its rivals. The most striking feature of the Mercedes was its full-width streamlined bodywork and its Achilles' heel the swing-axle rear suspension which endowed it with roadholding inferior to that of the Ferraris and Maseratis. Fangio's team-mates were Karl Kling and Hans Herrmann, both of whom were included in the team mainly for patriotic reasons.

At Reims, a debut carefully chosen because of its high-speed, flat-out characteristics well matched to those of the Mercedes, the German team annihilated the opposition. Fangio and Kling took the first two places and Herrmann set fastest lap before retiring. In an aura of gloom and despondency the Ferrari team next went to the British race at Silverstone. Although Fangio set fastest lap in practice, his car was exceedingly difficult to manage on this circuit with corners defined by oil drums; and while the Mercedes wallowed from corner to corner, clouting oil drum after oil drum, the Ferrari of Gonzalez evaporated into the distance. Then Moss with his

(*Above*) In the French race all the Ferrari works cars blew up their engines in their vain pursuit of the Mercedes. Gonzalez surveys his smoking 'Squalo'.

(*Below*) Ferrari's revenge came in the British race which Gonzalez won with this Tipo 625 car, a design that dated back to 1951.

private Maserati passed both Hawthorn and Fangio to take second place, only to retire with rear axle failure. Hawthorn also passed Fangio and before the finish Marimon slipped ahead to take third place for Maserati.

Practice for the German Grand Prix was marred by the fatal crash of Onofre Marimon and resulted in the withdrawal of the official Maserati team and his close friend Gonzalez was too dispirited to put up any sort of fight. Mercedes had responded to their Silverstone defeat by producing a new, unstreamlined version of the W.196 and this scored a decisive victory in the hands of Fangio. Fangio triumphed yet again at Bremgarten, but Gonzalez drove a fine race to take second place.

At Monza Mercedes reverted to the streamlined cars and Fangio won the race, but its real hero was Stirling Moss. So impressed had been the Maserati team by his performance at Silverstone that he had been invited to join the works team. He had retired at both the Nürburgring and at Bremgarten, but at Monza he forged ahead of Fangio and seemed all set for victory; he lost his lead when he was forced to stop to take on extra oil and retired shortly afterwards with a split oil tank. Fangio was the first to acknowledge that Moss was the moral victor and Mercedes only won this race by a very shaky margin. To round off the season was the last Spanish Grand Prix on the Pedralbes circuit. Here Mike Hawthorn with a 'Squalo' Ferrari – now fitted with coil spring front suspension – scored a fine victory, Luigi Musso's Maserati took second place and Fangio was third. At most races, in 1954, the Mercedes had dominated the results, but its successes were as much attributable to Fangio's skill as to its mechanical superiority.

One of the most significant features of the Spanish race had been the long-awaited appearance of the Lancia D.50 cars, which displayed a tremendous turn of speed, although lacking reliability at this stage in their career. Destined to be as successful as the Mercedes W.196, the D.50 was its complete antithesis and the ultimate in simplicity. It consisted of little more than the engine and gearbox with wheels and fuel tanks added, but, the work of the great Italian designer Vittorio Jano, it was also one of the most ingenious designs. The engine, which was a 90-degree V-8 of 2487 cc (73.6 × 73.1 mm) developing 260 bhp at 8000 rpm, was used as an integral stiffening member of the multi-tubular chassis, there was a de Dion rear axle and the 5-speed gearbox was in unit with the final drive. The fuel tanks were large panniers suspended on outriggers and Jano's idea was that, unlike a car with the tank mounted conventionally in the tail, the handling would not change as the fuel load was used up. At 1470 lb, the D.50 weighed substantially less than any of its rivals.

1955

Generally, the Mercedes team was well satisfied with the W.196. The team's hand was considerably strengthened by the addition of Stirling Moss, but this, in turn, depleted the Maserati team. Maserati then signed on Jean Behra as number one driver, but without Moss, much of Maserati's enthusiasm was lost, and the sole developments for 1955 were a new 5-speed gearbox and a streamlined version of the 250F which ran at Monza at the end of the season. The 553 re-appeared as the 555 'Super-Squalo' with a new chassis and restyled bodywork. The 625 was given coil spring front suspension, a 5-speed gearbox and restyled bodywork and was raced with the shorter stroke 'Super-Squalo' engine. One of Ferrari's biggest problems

(*Above*) The Lancia had a superb-looking V-8 engine with four twin-choke Solex carburetters mounted in the vee. (*Below*) At the 1954 Spanish race the compact, lithe Lancia D.50 distinguished by its pannier fuel tanks, made a long-awaited debut.

was a shortage of drivers, for Gonzalez, still not recovered from injuries sustained in a practice crash before the Tourist Trophy in September 1954, did not drive after the Argentinian races and Hawthorn had left to lead the British Vanwall team.

Although the new Connaught had been demonstrated to the press in August 1954, its first race was at the Easter Goodwood meeting. As brilliantly conceived as its Formula Two predecessor, the new B-series car had a 2470 cc (93.5 × 90 mm) Alta engine developing 240 bhp at 7000 rpm in a multi-tubular chassis with de Dion rear axle. The most striking feature of the new car, however, was its full-width streamlined body. It was more efficient aerodynamically than the Mercedes, the chassis was much more accessible as the upper part of the body lifted off in one piece and the driver's vision was better. In the latter part of the year the team decided to revert to conventional exposed-wheel bodywork because of the high cost of repairing the streamliners after minor accidents. Tony Vandervell had raced his 'Vanwall Special' consistently in 1954 and in the hands of Peter Collins it had shown great promise. For 1955 two cars, known simply as 'Vanwalls', were prepared. Hawthorn and Ken Wharton were signed up to drive them, but early in the season it became obvious that they were not as competitive as had been hoped and Hawthorn was released from his contract and returned to drive for Ferrari.

Even by South American standards the Argentinian Grand Prix was run in excessively hot conditions and only two drivers, both local men, were able to run through the race without relief. One was Juan Fangio who scored yet another victory for Mercedes and the other was Roberto Mieres who led the race at one stage, but finished fifth with his Maserati after a bout of fuel pump trouble. The complete Lancia team was eliminated in this race, but Ferrari 625 cars, each confusingly shared by three drivers because of the heat, took second and third places. The first European round was at Monaco – held after an interval of four years – where the favourites fell by the wayside and the winner was a complete outsider. After leading the race, Fangio was eliminated by a broken gearbox and Moss then assumed the lead only to retire when his car started to lay a dense smoke trail. Before Moss's retirement, Ascari in second place with his Lancia was almost a lap behind and striving desperately not to be lapped. He assumed first place on Moss's retirement without knowing it and on that very same lap his

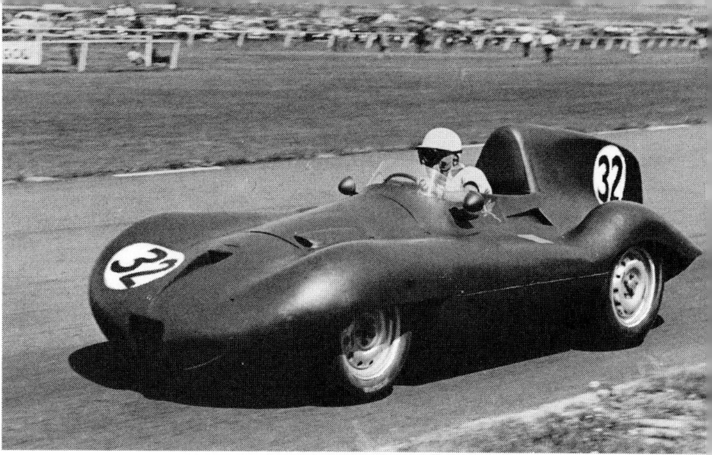

Bearers of British hopes: (*Left*) Tony Vandervell's Ferrari-inspired Vanwall in 1955 form with Ken Wharton at the wheel. (*Above*) The streamlined Connaught raced by the works in 1955 and seen there with Kenneth McAlpine at the wheel.

brakes locked up, the Lancia hit a bollard, bounced off the straw bales and plunged into Monte Carlo harbour. Ascari survived this terrifying incident, unhurt apart from a broken nose. As a result of these dramas Maurice Trintignant found himself in the lead with his 625 Ferrari and scored a very unexpected victory that was to prove Ferrari's only Championship win that season.

Ascari lost his life shortly afterwards when his Ferrari left the track and crashed at Monza for reasons that have never been satisfactorily explained. Already Lancia were in severe financial difficulties, and Ascari's death proved the final straw. The team withdrew from racing, but young Eugenio Castellotti, who had finished second at Monaco, was allowed to drive one of the cars as a private entrant in the next Championship race which was at Spa. Although he chased the Mercedes hard, the Italian was eliminated by gearbox trouble when in third place and the Stuttgart cars again dominated the results. The Spa race was on 5 June and on the following Saturday the flag fell for the start of the most tragic race in the history of motor racing. At Le Mans Pierre Levegh's Mercedes crashed into the spectator area and over eighty onlookers lost their lives. Although this was a sports car race, it had a profound effect on motor racing as a whole; the French, German, Swiss and Spanish Grands Prix were all cancelled; there was no more motor racing in France that year and it was banned for ever in Switzerland.

The next Championship round in a now depleted season was the Dutch Grand Prix at Zandvoort where Mercedes again took the first two places. Young Luigi Musso put up a very gallant fight with his Maserati and finished on the same lap as

A fine performance in the 1955 British race was turned in by young Luigi Musso who finished fifth with his Maserati 250F.

the Mercedes. The scene then switched to the smoke and grime of the Aintree circuit near Liverpool. Four Mercedes were entered in this race and they took the first four places with Stirling Moss winning on home ground. There was now no Championship round until the Italian race in September and this was held on the new combined road and banked track circuit. Here Amédée Gordini's new straight-eight car appeared, but it was disappointingly slow and ran last. Four Mercedes were entered, two streamlined (the only time in 1955 that these were used) and two unstreamlined. Two of the Mercedes retired, but Fangio and Taruffi still came home in the first two places. Not long after the British Grand Prix the entire Lancia team had been handed over to Ferrari for him to race under his own name. Three of the D.50s were entered at Monza, but they were withdrawn after practice because of tyre failures resulting from the strains of the banking.

At the end of 1955 Mercedes withdrew from both Grand Prix racing and sports car racing, having won five of the season's six Grand Prix races and every round of the Sports Car Championship the team had entered apart from Le Mans from which the two remaining cars were withdrawn after Levegh's terrible accident. The season closed on a definite note of optimism for supporters of the British racing green. In September B.R.M. revealed their new Type 25 car. The 4-cylinder 2497 cc (102.87 × 74.93 mm) engine developed 248 bhp at 9000 rpm and the car was squat, sturdy and purposeful-looking. If B.R.M. offered promise, Connaught had produced results. A team of two cars had been sent to the Syracuse Grand Prix in October and young dental student Tony Brooks at the wheel of the latest, unstreamlined Connaught scored a crushing victory over a strong team of works Maseratis. This was Britain's first victory in a Grand Prix proper since 1924 and marked the turning point in British Formula One fortunes.

1956

The retirement of Mercedes resulted in the two leading drivers of the day, Fangio and Moss, joining opposing teams. Fangio went to Ferrari where he stayed only for the one season. In 1956 Ferrari raced the Lancia D.50s which he progressively modified. The main change affected the pannier tanks which were now used to house only the exhaust pipes and the bulk of

(*Above*) This streamlined car was built by Maserati for the 1955 Italian Grand Prix. Jean Behra drove it into fourth place.

the fuel was carried in the tail. Ferrari had an immensely powerful team of drivers for, in addition to the World Champion, he signed on Peter Collins, Luigi Musso, Eugenio Castellotti and the Marquis de Portago. Olivier Gendebien also drove the Grand Prix cars occasionally.

Stirling Moss led the Maserati team and Behra stayed on as number two driver. Unchanged for the Argentinian race, the faithful 250F was modified as the season progressed and it remained one of the most successful Grand Prix cars. Of the British teams, B.R.M. signed on Mike Hawthorn, who lived in the hope of finding a British car that was really competitive, and Tony Brooks. For 1956 the Vanwalls were extensively modified and had a new multi-tubular chassis designed by Colin Chapman and a body of startling simplicity and aerodynamic efficiency which was the work of Frank Costin who designed Lotus bodies. Vanwall drivers were Harry Schell and Maurice Trintignant, but the team's only real success was to come in the *Daily Express* Trophy at Silverstone in May when Stirling Moss, in the absence of a works Maserati entry, drove for the team and scored a fine victory.

Although Fangio retired his own car with engine trouble in the Argentinian race, he took over Musso's and scored a victory over the Maseratis which seemed down on power. The tables were turned at Monaco where Moss led from start to finish and Fangio drove a ragged, untidy race well below his usual standard. Five Lancia-Ferraris were entered in the Belgian Grand Prix and after Moss's Maserati had lost a wheel when he was in second place, it seemed that Maranello would take the first four places. Both Castellotti and Fangio retired, however, with transmission trouble and a cheerful, grinning Peter

(*Below*) On test early in 1956 is the then new 4-cylinder B.R.M. with the team's number one driver, Mike Hawthorn, at the wheel.

Collins scored his first Championship victory. Moss took over Perdisa's car and had worked it up to third place by the finish.

The Maranello cars completely out-paced the Maseratis at Reims, but the car they could not lose was Harry Schell's Vanwall. After taking this car over from Hawthorn he came up through the field and battled with the four leading Lancia-Ferraris until forced to drop back with fuel-injection trouble. Fangio had to stop at the pits and Ferrari had instructed their drivers that at the end of lap 50 (eleven laps before the finish), the drivers would be shown the 'Stay as you are' signal. Collins was duelling with Castellotti for the lead, but he had friends in other pits who gave him advance warning of when lap 50 was approaching and on that lap he was able to ensure that he crossed the line first.

The Maseratis of Stirling Moss and private entrant Roy Salvadori each led the British Grand Prix, but both retired and again victory went to the Lancia-Ferraris. For Fangio, who had been having a very poor season, this was his first victory since the non-Championship Syracuse race. At the Nürburgring the Maseratis were outclassed and again victory went to Maranello. The Italian race, however, proved the most hectic of the season. The race was again held on the combined road and banked track circuit and the Lancia-Ferraris were again plagued by tyre troubles and also by failure of the steering arms. Castellotti and Musso both crashed – the latter whilst leading the race – and Peter Collins with a touch of chivalry handed over his second-place car to Juan Fangio, thereby ensuring that he gained his fourth World Championship. But Monza was a Maserati race and Moss scored a well-deserved victory.

(*Below, left*) 1956 was Fangio's only season with Ferrari. He is seen here in the British Grand Prix which provided his first victory since Syracuse early in the year.
(*Right*) Stirling Moss at the wheel of the Maserati 250F which he drove to victory in the 1956 Monaco race.

Battle of the blue – in the 1956 French Grand Prix Maurice Trintignant with the rear-engined Type 251 Bugatti leads Manzon's 8-cylinder Gordini. Both cars retired.

1957

For 1957 Juan Fangio joined the Maserati team which raced a further improved version of the 250F. This was similar to new cars that had appeared at Monza, but with much smaller tubing used for the chassis and long, low tapering nose. The company was also working on a new and very potent V-12 engine to fit into the existing chassis, but this version did not run in a Championship race until the end of the season. Ferrari continued to race the Lancia-Ferraris which in their 1957 form with the pannier tanks removed altogether and the exhausts exposed were known as the Tipo 801. After a thoroughly unhappy and unsuccessful season in 1956 with B.R.M., Hawthorn rejoined the Ferrari team. His team-mates were Peter Collins, Luigi Musso and, after Eugenio Castellotti had been killed in a testing crash, Maurice Trintignant. The most significant re-arrangement of drivers was at Vanwall where Stirling Moss became team-leader, backed up by Tony Brooks. The cars now had coil spring rear suspension and, with 290 bhp at their disposal, were the most powerful cars racing. Both Connaught and Gordini retired from racing early in the season because of financial difficulties. After a disastrous season in which both Hawthorn and Brooks miraculously escaped from crashes caused by mechanical failure, the B.R.M. team enjoyed an equally dismal 1957 with the cars plagued by mechanical troubles and few drivers were willing to chance their arm with the Bourne machinery. As yet modestly, a new force was rising in Grand Prix racing, the Formula Two Cooper, which ran in some Grands Prix with the capacity of its Climax engine increased from 1475 cc to 1960 cc.

Probably the most significant feature of the 1957 season was the manner in which the Lancia-Ferraris were outclassed by the latest Maseratis and Vanwalls. Vanwall did not run in the Argentinian Grand Prix and Maseratis took the first three places. As in 1950, the Monaco race was marred by a multi-car crash that eliminated several of the leading contenders and Juan Fangio scored an easy victory from Tony Brooks' Vanwall. There was no Belgian or Dutch race in 1957 and the French race at Rouen proved a Fangio benefit. Both Moss and Brooks were unfit to race at Rouen and their places were taken by Stuart Lewis-Evans and Roy Salvadori. So impressed was Tony Vandervell by the performance of Lewis-Evans in this race and the non-Championship Reims Grand Prix, that he decided henceforth to field a third car for him.

Both Moss and Brooks were back in the Vanwall team at the European Grand Prix at Aintree and from the fall of the flag Moss drew steadily away in the lead from Jean Behra's Maserati. Magneto trouble eliminated the leader and Brooks was called in to hand over to Moss. By the time Moss had rejoined the race, the Vanwall was in ninth place and apparently with very little chance of finishing in the first three. Moss carved his way through the field, moving up to fourth place on the retirements of Collins and Fangio and taking third place from team-mate Lewis-Evans. Then the Vanwall team benefited from the misfortunes of others; the leading Maserati of Behra blew up its engine, scattering debris all over the track, and second-place man Hawthorn punctured a tyre on parts of the

Vanwall vindication: after four seasons of unsuccessful effort, Tony Vandervell's Vanwall scored a fine victory in the 1957 European Grand Prix at Aintree. Stirling Moss and Lewis-Evans are seen when in first and second places.

Maserati's clutch and was forced to stop for a wheel-change. Moss swept into the lead and went on to take Britain's first Championship victory and first win in a National Grand Prix since Segrave won the French race in 1923.

At the Nürburgring the Vanwalls suffered suspension problems and victory went to Fangio's Maserati which came through after a refuelling stop to take the lead from the Lancia-Ferraris of Hawthorn and Collins. Because of the cancellation of other races, Italy was allowed to stage two rounds in the Championship in 1957 and the additional race was the Pescara Grand Prix held on a magnificent 25-kilometre road circuit with difficult mountainous stretches and a fast straight. Although Luigi Musso's very well driven Lancia-Ferrari led for the first two laps, Moss then forged ahead with the Vanwall and scored yet another fine victory. The Monza race was held on the road circuit only and the race provided a tremendous battle between the Vanwalls and Maseratis. Behra with the new V-12 Maserati and Fangio each led the race for a while, but Moss took the lead and, drawing out an advantage of over 40 seconds, scored Vanwall's third Championship victory of the season.

1958

A sad blow to motor racing was the withdrawal of Maserati at the end of 1957, a decision taken because of the very high costs of their racing programme and because of losses incurred when the Argentinian government defaulted on commitments after the fall of the Peron régime. Juan Fangio had also decided to retire, but neither he nor Maserati were quite finished with Formula One racing and neither took their final bow until the 1958 French Grand Prix. 250F cars continued to be raced by private owners, however, right until the end of the Formula.

For 1958 Grand Prix cars were compelled to run on 'Avgas' aviation fuel, an unsatisfactory compromise resulting from the oil companies' desire that cars should use ordinary pump fuel to increase advertising benefits and the manufacturers expressing reluctance to cease using alcohol-based fuels. Adapting existing engines was difficult and expensive and Vanwall only achieved this at the cost of a reduced power output of 262 bhp at 7500 rpm and increased mechanical fragility because of the loss of the cooling properties of alcohol. For 1958 the Vanwall team of drivers was unchanged.

Ferrari had now abandoned the Lancia-based cars and raced the new Dino 246 model. The V-6 twin overhead camshaft Dino had first appeared in 1957 in 1489 cc Formula Two form, but by 1958 the cars had 2417 cc (85 × 71 mm) engines developing a claimed 290 bhp at 8300 rpm. Ferrari had a strong team of drivers headed by Hawthorn, Collins and Musso with the German von Trips, the American Phil Hill and the Belgian Olivier Gendebien available as and when required.

It was indicative of the changing face of motor racing that the other three contenders in racing in 1958 were British and two were powered by Coventry-Climax engines. The Cooper works team fielded cars for Jack Brabham and Roy Salvadori, while Rob Walker's car was driven by Maurice Trintignant. The Lotus approach to racing was rather more scientific and Colin Chapman's front-engined Climax-powered design featured an elaborate space-frame, his famous 'strut' rear suspension and a 5-speed gearbox in unit with the final drive. Lotus ran only in Formula Two events in 1957, but their cars with enlarged engines appeared at most of the 1958 Championship rounds. Although they were still very unreliable, B.R.M. persevered with their 4-cylinder cars and the team now had to its credit wins in the poorly supported 1957 Caen Grand Prix and *Daily Express* Trophy race. Power output of the B.R.M. on 'Avgas' was 270 bhp and the team's drivers were Jean Behra and Harry Schell.

(*Above*) Duel at Monza, 1957: in the opening laps the Vanwalls of Lewis-Evans, Brooks and Moss lead from the Maseratis of Fangio and Masten Gregory.

(*Right*) A lightweight 'Piccolo' Maserati 250F, one of two raced by the American Scuderia Buell team in 1958.

The Argentinian race in January was poorly supported and the Vanwall, Cooper and B.R.M. teams were all absent. This did, however, mean that Stirling Moss was free to drive a 1960 cc Cooper for Rob Walker and opposition came from the works Ferraris and Fangio's Maserati. Fangio lost the lead through tyre trouble and the Ferraris were handling badly. Moss drove at a steady pace, conserving his tyres, for not only was his pit desperately short of spares, but the team was concerned about the delay in changing the Cooper's bolt-on wheels. So the tortoise sneaked into the lead and although in the closing stages of the race Moss was driving on the grass and through patches of oil to save the tyres, he took the chequered flag a hundred yards ahead of Luigi Musso's Ferrari.

Then came the Monaco race where a total of five Coopers was entered and Walker's Argentine-winner driven by Trintignant had a 2014 cc engine. All three works Vanwalls retired, as did the Ferrari of Hawthorn. Trintignant swept into the lead and the efforts of the three remaining Ferraris of Musso, Collins and von Trips were in vain. It was now clearly established that the Cooper was a serious force to be reckoned with.

At Zandvoort the three Vanwalls were fastest in practice and the Ferraris were unable to match their speed on this circuit. In the race two of the British cars retired, but Moss led throughout to win from the works B.R.M.s of Schell and Behra which ran better than on any previous occasion in their unhappy career. In the Spa race, Moss took the lead for Vanwall in the race, but retired on the first lap when he missed a gear, the engine over-revved and a valve bent. Brooks then went in front and stayed in the lead to the finish.

Juan Fangio made his first appearance since the Argentinian race and last ever when he drove at Reims the new lightweight 'Piccolo' Maserati, in fact a works entry but ostensibly privately entered. Mike Hawthorn drove his Dino magnificently and led the race from start to finish, but his victory was marred by the death of Luigi Musso who lost control on a fast bend and crashed. It was much the same story at Silverstone where the Vanwalls, even with Moss driving at his hardest, could make no impression on the leading Ferrari of Peter Collins, and after Moss had retired, his sleek green car laying a thick trail of smoke, Hawthorn took second place.

Next on the calendar was the German race. After their failure at the circuit in 1957, the Vanwall team had learnt the error of its ways and suspension modifications ensured that the British cars handled at the Nürburgring as well as any of the opposition. Moss went straight into the lead at the start of the race and drew away from the Ferraris until magneto trouble brought about his retirement. Tony Brooks was now third behind the Ferraris of Hawthorn and Collins, but he succeeded in passing them both; Peter Collins tragically lost his life when, taking a bend on opposite-lock as he had on every preceding lap, he made an error of judgment and crashed. A very saddened Hawthorn was relieved to retire when his clutch gave trouble on the following lap and Salvadori's 2.2-litre Cooper took second place.

An addition to the Championship in 1958 was the Portuguese Grand Prix held at Porto. Although Hawthorn led in the opening stages of the race, Moss then went ahead and won the race for Vanwall.

The Italian race saw another furious duel between the Ferrari and Vanwall teams. The Vanwalls went ahead at the start, then they were passed by Phil Hill's Ferrari, but when this threw a tyre tread, Moss went back into the lead. Both Moss and Lewis-Evans retired, Brooks stopped at the pits because of an oil leak and then rejoined the race in third place. The Vanwall driver soon caught Phil Hill and set off in pursuit of the leading Ferrari of Mike Hawthorn. Brooks' chance came when the Dino slowed with clutch trouble and he went ahead to win by 22 seconds.

A final round in the Championship was still to be held, the Moroccan Grand Prix at Ain-Diab which was of crucial importance as far as the Drivers' Championship was concerned.

The leader, Mike Hawthorn, had scored 40 points from six races. Stirling Moss had finished only in five races and from these he had scored 32 points. If he won at Ain-Diab and made fastest lap, he would gain a further 9 points and clinch the Championship – unless Hawthorn finished second and would then substitute the score of six points for one of the events he had already counted in his total. Moss drove one of the finest races of his career, winning and setting fastest lap, but Hawthorn took second place and thereby pipped Moss for the Championship by one point. A sad blow to motor racing was the death of Lewis-Evans from burns sustained when his Vanwall crashed. Mike Hawthorn decided to retire from racing, but was killed shortly afterwards in a road accident at the wheel of his Jaguar.

(*Above*) Where the road circuit sweeps under the banked track at Monza, the Vanwalls of Moss and Lewis-Evans lead the eventual winner, Tony Brooks and Mike Hawthorn.

(*Opposite, top*) Harry Schell driving the 1958 B.R.M. in the German Grand Prix. (*Middle row*) Mike Hawthorn in his V-6 Dino Ferrari in the 1958 Spa race. (*Bottom*) Tony Brooks, the victor of the 1958 Belgian Grand Prix, in his Vanwall.

(*Above*) Fast, but fragile, the Lotus 16, nick-named the 'Mini-Vanwall', is driven here by Graham Hill in the 1959 Italian Grand Prix.

(*Right*) Another new model raced in 1959 was the Aston Martin DBR4, seen here at Monza, with Roy Salvadori at the wheel.

1959

In January 1959 came the shock announcement that Tony Vandervell had decided to withdraw from racing for health reasons. For two glorious season the Vanwall team had been at the forefront of Grand Prix racing and had gained more success than had ever before been achieved by a British racing team. Vandervell continued development work on a very limited scale and cars made occasional appearances, but they were never again to achieve success. British Grand Prix hopes now rested with the Cooper, B.R.M. and Lotus teams. In 1959 both Cooper and Lotus used a new version of the Coventry-Climax engine with a full capacity of 2495 cc (94 × 89.9 mm) and developing 240 bhp at 6750 rpm. Although this was a less powerful engine than that used by the teams' rivals, the low weight and superb handling of the Cooper more than compensated for this power deficiency on all except the very fastest circuits. Cooper's hand was much strengthened by Stirling Moss driving a car for Rob Walker, but Moss also had at his disposal a B.R.M. made specially available by Owen Organisation chief Sir Alfred Owen. This was entered in the name of the British Racing Partnership and painted in the team's pale green finish. It came to an untimely end however when it crashed badly in the German Grand Prix with Hans Herrmann at the wheel.

A new British contender in 1959 was the Aston Martin developed from the team's very successful sports car practice.

Lower and lighter, the 1959 version of the Ferrari Dino with Dan Gurney at the wheel in the Portuguese Grand Prix.

Unfortunately it was outdated when it appeared and failed to achieve any success despite the efforts of drivers Roy Salvadori and Carroll Shelby. The 1959 Ferrari Dino had Dunlop disc brakes. Maranello had a strong team of drivers consisting of Tony Brooks, Phil Hill, Jean Behra and ex-Lotus man Cliff Allison.

There was no Argentinian race in 1959 and so the first round of the Championship was at Monaco. Jean Behra set the pace until his Ferrari's engine blew up and then Moss at the wheel of Rob Walker's Cooper took the lead. Again the lead changed when Moss retired with final drive trouble and Jack Brabham with a works Cooper was the winner. After a race-long duel with the Coopers, Joakim Bonnier won the Dutch Grand Prix for B.R.M. – for both driver and car it was the first Championship win – and, as in 1958, the Ferraris were no match for the British cars on this circuit. The Reims race was one of two during the 1959 season in which the Ferraris won on sheer speed and Tony Brooks and Phil Hill took the first two places for Maranello.

Ferrari did not run in the British Grand Prix and Brabham with his works Cooper scored another fine victory from Moss's B.R.M. The German Grand Prix was run in two heats on the dangerous banked Avus track at Berlin. Again the Coopers lacked the speed of the Ferraris and Dinos driven by Brooks, Dan Gurney and Phil Hill took the first three places. The

superiority of Cooper roadholding prevailed in the Portuguese race on the Monsanto circuit at Lisbon and Moss scored an easy victory. It had been expected that Ferrari speed would win the Italian Grand Prix for Maranello, but Moss at the wheel of the Cooper played a wily game and won from Phil Hill. The last round in the Championship was another addition to the series, the United States Grand Prix at Sebring. Number two driver in the Cooper team Bruce McLaren scored his first Championship win after Brabham had run out of fuel.

(*Above*) World Champion in action: Jack Brabham and his Cooper-Climax in the 1959 British Grand Prix at Aintree which he won.

1960

The implications of the successes of the rear-engined Coopers had not been lost on the team's rivals and at the 1959 Italian race there had appeared in practice a new rear-engined B.R.M. It was a development of this car that the Bourne team used in the 1960 Championship races apart from the Argentinian

(*Opposite*) Jack Brabham won the Drivers' Championship at the wheel of a Cooper in 1960 for the second year in succession.

Grand Prix at the beginning of the year. B.R.M. drivers were Joakim Bonnier, Graham Hill (who had left the Lotus team) and Dan Gurney (from Ferrari). Ferrari was now thinking ahead and concentrating on developing cars for the new Formula of 1961 onwards and contented himself with fitting a new wishbone independent rear suspension to the Dinos and using a modified 5-speed gearbox.

Throughout 1959 Colin Chapman had struggled to make his front-engined cars raceworthy, but he realised that it was a hopeless battle and followed the fashion by introducing a rear-engined car for 1960. The Lotus 18 was of very simple concept, but it had a superbly designed multi-tubular space-frame, new transverse link rear suspension and a dry weight of only 6 cwt. In addition to the works cars driven by Ireland, Stacey and Clark, one was delivered to Rob Walker for Moss to drive. The 1960 version of the Cooper had coil-spring rear suspension and a 5-speed gearbox. As well as the Climax-powered cars, others with Maserati engines were raced by private owners and the Italian Scuderia Eugenio Castellotti ran the so-called Cooper-Castellotti cars powered by Ferrari 'Squalo' engines dating back to 1954–5. Aston Martin continued to race their front-engined DBR4/250 cars in the early part of the year, but these were now so hopelessly outclassed that the team pulled out of racing in mid-season.

CASTROL
FERODO
LUCAS
9

LUCAS
4

McLaren's Cooper won the Argentinian Grand Prix and at Monaco, the potential of the Lotus 18 was shown by Stirling Moss who scored a fine victory with the Rob Walker car. At Zandvoort the tables were turned and Brabham won, but he had been hotly pursued by Moss until the Lotus driver lost a lot of time in the pits having a damaged wheel changed.

Tragedy struck the Lotus team at the Belgian race. Moss crashed in practice as the result of losing a rear wheel and his injuries were bad enough to put him out of racing until the Portuguese race in August and works driver Alan Stacey was killed when he crashed during the race, probably as a result of being struck in the face by a bird. The only challenge to Brabham came from Phil Hill's Ferrari, but after a broken pipe leading to the fuel pressure gauge had caused the American to stop at the pits, the Cooper driver scored an easy victory. Development work on the Climax engine had endowed the Coopers with sufficient speed to match the Ferraris even on the fast Reims course and in the French race Brabham scored yet another victory. Another Cooper victory followed at Silverstone. The German race was held for Formula Two cars in 1960 and so the next Championship round was the Portuguese race at Porto. Moss stopped at the pits with a mis-firing engine; young John Surtees was leading the race comfortably with his works Lotus when he retired because of fuel leaking on to the pedals and so the race reverted to the very familiar pattern of Jack Brabham winning from team-mate McLaren.

In 1960 the Italian race was held on the combined road and track circuit at Monza and the British constructors declined to enter as they maintained that their cars were not designed for track racing. The organisers decided to go ahead without the British teams and made up the entry with Formula Two cars. The result was a walk-over for the Ferrari team which took the first three places with Cabianca's Ferrari-engined Cooper-Castellotti fourth and a works Formula Two Ferrari fifth. The final race of the season was the United States Grand Prix where Moss scored a fine victory with his Rob Walker-entered Lotus.

So, one of the most successful of all racing Formulae came to an end and the United States Grand Prix marked the end of an era which had seen the decline of Italian racing fortunes and the rise to power of the British constructors, a revolution in racing car design and some of the closest duels that racing has ever witnessed.

(*Opposite top*) Following in Cooper's wheel-tracks, Colin Chapman produced the rear-engined Lotus 18 for 1960. In the British Grand Prix, John Surtees finished second at the wheel of a works entry.

(*Bottom*) The highlight of the 1960 race at Silverstone was Graham Hill's drive through the field after a bad start. He took the lead only to spin off and retire.

Jim Clark was the most inspired driver of the early 1960s. He is seen here with the new and improved Lotus 33 in 1964.

CHAPTER FOUR

An Era of British Domination, 1961-5

1961

HAVING ridden on a wave of success since 1957, the British constructors were strongly opposed to the introduction of the new Grand Prix Formula and, confident that they could persuade the Fédération Internationale de l'Automobile to change its mind, they made no attempts to develop engines for the new Formula. Eventually they realised that they had lost the fight and both B.R.M. and Coventry-Climax put work in hand on new V-8 1500 cc units; for the first season, however, all the British teams, including B.R.M., were forced to rely on the 4-cylinder 1475 cc Climax unit that had first appeared in 1957 for Formula Two racing. As a result the 1961 season proved a Ferrari benefit. Both Cooper and B.R.M. used chassis similar to those of their 1960 cars, while Lotus produced a new, more compact and more aerodynamic car, the 21. A new British marque was the Emeryson, built by Paul Emery, and two of these cars were raced by the Équipe Nationale Belge.

By late 1960 Ferrari was racing a very well sorted rear-engined Formula Two car with a V-6 engine of 1476 cc (73 × 58.8 mm) having the cylinders at an angle of 65 degrees. In its 1961 form this car, known as the Tipo 156, developed 180 bhp at 9000 rpm, and this meant that it was around 30 bhp more powerful than its British rivals. Both this car and the improved version with the cylinders at 120 degrees were the work of designer Carlo Chiti and were distinguished by a unique 'twin-nostril' nose section. The advantages of the slightly later 120-degree version were greater reliability at higher engine speeds and an even higher power output of 190 bhp. Ferrari had a very strong team of drivers in 1961 consisting of Phil Hill, Wolfgang von Trips and Richie Ginther, but other drivers were also entered in some races.

(*Above, top*) Moss won the 1961 Monaco Grand Prix with this 1960 Lotus fitted with a 4-cylinder Coventry-Climax engine.

(*Bottom*) At Reims, all three works Ferraris were eliminated. Ginther's lies abandoned in the foreground.

(*Opposite*) A fortnight before he lost his life at the Nürburging in 1958, Peter Collins scored a brilliant victory with his Ferrari Dino in the British Grand Prix.

A new contender in Grand Prix racing was the German Porsche team, who had built very successful Formula Two cars. Like Cooper, Porsche had always been advocates of the rear-engine layout and their single-seater with flat-four air-cooled 1498 cc (85 × 66 mm) engine developing around 160 bhp was no exception.

In an even worse position than the works teams was Rob Walker, who had wanted to buy one of the latest Lotus 21s, but was not allowed to do so because of fuel contract difficulties. So Stirling Moss drove his old 1960 Lotus 18, distinguished later in the year by a more streamlined nose section. At Monaco Moss, after taking the lead on lap 14, drove admirably, heading the trio of Ferraris to the finish. A bare eight days later was the Dutch race at Zandvoort. The only driver to seriously worry the two leading Ferraris was Jim Clark with the new Lotus 21, but they gradually drew away from him, while Moss, was fourth ahead of the third Ferrari driven by Richie Ginther.

As at Zandvoort, Ferrari fielded three of the 120-degree V-6 cars at Spa for his usual drivers, but a 65-degree car was painted yellow and loaned to the Équipe Nationale Belge for one-time works driver Olivier Gendebien to handle. On this high-speed circuit the three works cars were fastest in practice and Maranello took the first four places in the race with the under-powered British cars unable to put up any sort of fight.

At Reims, the works Ferraris went straight into the lead at the start, but Stirling Moss moved up to third place when Ginther spun. Ginther re-passed Moss and stale-mate was reached with Moss simply lacking the power to challenge the Italian cars, and then he began to drop back with brake trouble. The first Ferrari failure came when von Trips pulled into the pits to retire with engine trouble; then Moss lost four laps while a brake pipe was replaced. When Hill spun and stalled on tar melted by the very strong sunshine, he was clouted by Moss's Lotus with the result that the British car was out of the race with broken suspension and Hill lost a lot of time trying to restart his car. So only the one works Ferrari remained out in front and that was eliminated when Ginther was forced to abandon it on the circuit with engine trouble. The lead was now being fought out between the very inexperienced Giancarlo Baghetti in a privately entered Ferrari and Dan Gurney and Joakim Bonnier at the wheel of works Porsche entries. On the very last lap Gurney was leading when Baghetti pulled out of

American Phil Hill won the 1961 Drivers' Championship.

his slip-stream 300 yards before the finishing line and snatched victory by a tenth of a second. This was a most exciting French Grand Prix and a magnificent victory by a novice driver.

A new car to appear at the British Grand Prix at Aintree was the experimental front-engined four-wheel-drive Ferguson. This was entered in the name of the Rob Walker team and driven by Jack Fairman. After a pit-stop the car was push-started and this resulted in its disqualification. Even so the car was taken over by Moss after the retirement of his Lotus and he lapped serenely and swiftly until the organisers had received so many protests about a disqualified car still being out on the circuit, that the Ferguson was called in and withdrawn. The race proved another Maranello benefit and Ferraris took the first three places. The tables were turned at the Nürburgring where Moss once again displayed his mastery and led throughout with his outdated, underpowered car, while the Ferraris of von Trips and Phil Hill trailed home in second and third places.

The Italian Grand Prix, was marred by a horrible accident that cost the life of the potential World Champion, Wolfgang von Trips. On the second lap he collided with Clark's Lotus and while the British car merely spun on to the grass, by some terrible whim of fate, the Ferrari launched itself up the bank, throwing the driver out and killing eleven spectators who were leaning against the wire-mesh fence. After Monza Phil Hill had an unassailable lead in the Drivers' Championship and

Ferrari decided not to contest the United States Grand Prix, now held at Watkins Glen. This was won by Innes Ireland and this was the first Championship victory by either the driver or Team Lotus.

(*Opposite*) Dan Gurney at the wheel of the 4-cylinder Porsche in the 1961 German Grand Prix.

1962

For the coming season there was a considerable reorganisation amongst the racing teams. Ferrari lost most of his top technicians together with team manager Tavoni when they left en masse after a major disagreement. The Ferraris were changed in detail only and Ferrari had four drivers under contract, Phil Hill, Ricardo Rodriguez, Giancarlo Baghetti and Lorenzo Bandini. Jack Brabham had parted company with the Cooper team which was now led by Bruce McLaren and the Australian raced private Lotus cars until the new Brabham with V-8 Climax engine was ready to race.

At Lotus, Ireland had been replaced by Trevor Taylor. Early in the season there appeared the new Lotus 24 with Climax V-8 engine, but this was intended primarily as a car for private owners and at the Dutch Grand Prix a further new

(*Overleaf*) (*Left*) Phil Hill spinning his Ferrari Dino in the 1960 Monaco Grand Prix. He rejoined the race to finish third. (*Right*) On the banking at Monza in 1961 is the V-6 rear-engined Ferrari of Richie Ginther.

The 1962 version of the V-6 Ferrari failed to repeat the successes of the previous year.

ENERGOL
BP
BP
ENERGO
36

I II III
GIRI
AGIP

model was introduced. This was the revolutionary 25 model with a monocoque chassis built according to aircraft design principles and with the engine exceptionally accessible and the chassis also forming the lower part of the body. A new British car was the space-frame Climax-powered Lola designed by Eric Broadley and two of these cars were entered by the Bowmaker-Yeoman team for John Surtees and Roy Salvadori to drive.

B.R.M. now had their V-8 cars fully raceworthy and these were driven by Graham Hill and Richie Ginther. Twelve months later than was originally anticipated, the new flat-eight Porsche was ready and Dan Gurney and Joakim Bonnier continued to drive for the Stuttgart team. Stirling Moss was recovering from his serious crash at the 1962 Easter Goodwood meeting and was destined never to race again.

Hill scored a fine victory with his B.R.M. in the first round of the Championship at Zandvoort – the team's second after twelve years in Grand Prix racing – and he was leading at Monaco when his engine broke only seven laps before the chequered flag. The result was a victory for Bruce McLaren, and Phil Hill's second place with a Ferrari was to prove the best Maranello performance of a very unsuccessful season. By the Spa race the Lotus 25 had found its form and Jim Clark scored a very fine victory for Team Lotus with Graham Hill crossing the finishing line over forty seconds behind. In 1962 the French race was held on the difficult and testing Rouen circuit and the winner was not one of the favoured British entries. Dan Gurney's rather sluggard Porsche scored the make's

(*Above*) Jim Clark drove the new monocoque Lotus 25 during 1962 and won three Championship races including the British Grand Prix.

(*Left*) Consistent performers in 1962 were Bruce McLaren and the Cooper-Climax V-8, seen here in the British race.

(*Overleaf*) (*Top*) In the 1962 British race Dan Gurney drove a works 8-cylinder Porsche. (*Bottom*) In the same race, Jim Clark, the winner, drove a Lotus 25-Coventry-Climax. Here he laps the 4-cylinder Porsche of de Beaufort.

one and only Championship victory, crossing the line a lap ahead of the works Cooper of Tony Maggs. But this had been a victory by default, and by the British race at Aintree the customary British speed and reliability had re-asserted itself and Jim Clark was the winner from Surtees' Lola, a combination that was ever improving.

The German race at the Nürburgring was held on a wet track and, although Gurney seized an initial lead with the sleek, silver Porsche, he was passed by both Graham Hill and John Surtees. In 1962 the Italian race was held on the road circuit only and yet again neither the Porsches nor the Ferraris had the speed to match the V-8 British cars. At the Monza race the Lotus 25s had been plagued by trouble with their German-

54

8

20

built ZF gearboxes, but this had been overcome by the United States race and Clark, who went straight into the lead at the start of the race, scored a well deserved victory from Graham Hills' B.R.M. Ferrari ran neither in this race nor in the South African Grand Prix, the latest addition to the series, held on 29th December. Another absentee was the Porsche team, which retired from racing at the end of the 1962 season. This race was completely dominated by Jim Clark with his Lotus 25 until three-quarters race distance, when a bolt dropped out of the Climax engine, which lost most of its oil. As a result, the victor was again Graham Hill who also won the Drivers' Championship.

(*Above*) Most promising newcomer in 1962 was the Lola designed by Eric Broadley and entered by the Bowmaker team. Here John Surtees is at the wheel in the British race in which he finished second.

(*Below*) B.R.M. finally achieved substantial success in 1962. Graham Hill is seen in the German Grand Prix which he won.

1963

The British constructors had every reason to be pleased with the way their cars had performed in 1962 and few modifications were made for the coming season. It was clear, however, that the Cooper star was waning and that their place as the dominant British team had been usurped by B.R.M. with Lotus achieving almost equal success. Now that Porsche had withdrawn from racing, Dan Gurney joined the Brabham team, and Joakim Bonnier drove for Rob Walker what had been a 1962 works Cooper. The British offensive was strengthened by the introduction of a MK II version of the Coventry-Climax engine with shorter stroke, the ability to rev up to 10,000 rpm and Lucas fuel injection. The Bowmaker-Yeoman team decided to withdraw from racing notwithstanding the tremendous potential displayed by the Lola. John Surtees joined the Ferrari team, the second Ferrari driver being Belgian Willy Mairesse. For the time being Ferrari continued to rely on the V-6 cars.

The results at Monaco indicated that B.R.M. and Lotus were going to maintain their 1962 form, for the Bourne cars took the first two places and Jim Clark had led with his Lotus until the gearbox seized up. Thereafter Lotus became supreme and Jim Clark won the Belgian, Dutch, French and British races in succession. Hill's B.R.M. was the victim of gearbox trouble at Spa and although Graham had been in second place, he had been unable to match the speed of the flying Scot. It had been much the same story at Zandvoort where Hill gained second place after a battle with Jack Brabham only to come into the pits when his engine overheated. At Silverstone Hill drove a 1962 car and after a race-long duel with the Ferrari of

John Surtees he ran out of fuel on the last lap and dropped to third place behind the Italian car.

John Surtees appeared at the wheel of a new and much improved Ferrari at the Italian Grand Prix. Designed to take Ferrari's new V-8 engine which was not yet ready, the new car had instead a modified version of the familiar V-6. The chassis was a monocoque structure and the front suspension had been derived from Lotus practice. Hill led the race with his B.R.M. initially, but was passed by both Surtees and Clark. Surtees just held off the Scot until lap 17 when the Ferrari's engine blew up in a cloud of white smoke and Clark went on to score his fifth Championship victory of the season. B.R.M. fielded 1962 cars in the United States Grand Prix and although they dominated the results, the Bourne cars by no means dominated the race itself.

Champion combination: Jim Clark and the Lotus 25 in the 1963 Dutch Grand Prix which he won at 97.53 mph.

1964

Colin Chapman had every reason to be well pleased with the performance of the Lotus 25 and contented himself with a series of detailed changes which resulted in the model becoming known as the 33. Jim Clark remained as team-leader, but he was joined by Peter Arundell and Team Lotus also had the services of Mike Spence as and when required. The 1963 semi-monocoque B.R.M. had proved a partial failure and there appeared a new car from Bourne which retained the centre monocoque section, but also had stressed-skin extensions running the length of the car and the engine and gearbox were bolted on directly. Cooper endeavoured to combat their waning fortunes by producing a new and very light car based on their Formula Three model, with the multi-tubular space-frame strengthened by welding sheet steel panels round the centre-section. Bruce McLaren remained as team-leader, but his number two, young American Tim Mayer, was killed in a practice crash during the Tasman races and his place was taken by Phil Hill. Ferrari had ready for the coming season his 1487 cc (64×57.8 mm) V-8 engine developing 220 bhp at 1100 rpm, but while Surtees drove this throughout the year, Bandini had to make do with a V-6 until the Italian race.

Jim Clark was clearly the most outstanding driver of the era and at Monaco he led easily, increasing his lead even after the rear torsional stabilising bar broke. As the organisers were

(*Overleaf*) (*Left*) Graham Hill and Jim Clark at Silverstone in 1964. (*Right*) The outstanding driver of the years 1962–5 was Jim Clark who won the Drivers' Championship twice. Here he is seen with his Lotus 33-Coventry-Climax in the 1964 British Grand Prix which he won.

J. CLARK

Dutch Grand Prix, 1963: Richie Ginther (B.R.M.) leads Joakim Bonnier (Cooper), Dan Gurney (Brabham) and Peter Arundell (Lotus).

considering 'black-flagging' the Lotus for trailing the bar, Chapman called him in for it to be cut away. By the time Clark had rejoined the race, he had dropped to third place behind Hill's B.R.M. and Gurney's Brabham. When Gurney retired with gearbox failure, Clark moved up a place, but loss of oil pressure caused his retirement near the end of the race – even so, under F.I.A. regulations he was classified as taking fourth place. Clark had better luck at Zandvoort and led the

(*Right*) Phil Hill in the 1963 Belgian Grand Prix with the Italian A.T.S. car.

(*Below*) In the 1963 British Grand Prix at Silverstone Graham Hill with the V-8 B.R.M. laps Keith Greene's Gilby.

Super National
DAILY EXPRESS
GIRL G
HILL
3
CLARK
TEAM LOTUS
5

(*Opposite*) The starting grid of the 1965 British Grand Prix with Jim Clark in his Lotus 33 (*nearest the camera*) and Graham Hill in a B.R.M.

(*Right*) John Surtees at the wheel of the lower and sleeker version of the V-6 Ferrari in the 1963 British race.

(*Below*) Jim Clark, World Champion in 1963 and 1965, who tragically lost his life in a Formula Two crash at Hockenheim early in 1968.

In 1964 former World Champion Phil Hill signed up with the Cooper team. He is seen seated in the team's new car with the tubular chassis reinforced by spot welding the side panels to the main structure.

(*Opposite, top*) Dan Gurney and the Climax-powered Brabham, seen here in the 1964 British race, were always a serious force to reckon with.

(*Bottom*) New faces in Grand Prix racing: the Japanese team of 12-cylinder cars at the 1965 French Grand Prix. No. 28 is driven by Ronnie Bucknum and No. 26 by Richie Ginther.

race throughout, but indicative of the resurgent power of Ferrari was Surtees' second place with a V-8 car.

At the Belgian race, Jim Clark's Lotus snatched the race after the Brabham of Gurney had run out of fuel.

1964 was the seventieth anniversary of the first motoring competition, the Paris-Rouen run of 1894, so it was appropriate that the French Grand Prix should be run on the fine Rouen circuit. It was even more appropriate that the winner should be Dan Gurney. The British race was held for the first time at Brands Hatch and Clark won yet again.

A new car to appear at the German Grand Prix was the Japanese Honda, powered by a V-12 engine mounted transversely – a layout reminiscent of the 1956 Bugatti Type 251. Surtees scored a fine victory at the Nürburgring, but he had to fight hard for it, staving off Clark's Lotus until it was passed by Gurney's Brabham and then only pulling away from the Brabham when it was slowed by overheating. Also held in August was the one and only Austrian Grand Prix on the very rough and bumpy Zeltweg airfield circuit. Mechanical troubles eliminated all the favourites and Lorenzo Bandini scored an unexpected victory with his Ferrari V-6 car. The Italian race developed into a duel between Surtees and Gurney with Clark keeping a watching brief in third spot, and the Ferrari driver scored his second Championship race victory of the season.

The teams now crossed the Atlantic to compete in the United States and Mexican races. Surtees drove one of the usual V-8 cars at Watkins Glen, but Bandini had the new flat-12 car that had appeared in practice at Monza. Jim Clark made a brilliant start and drew away from the rest of the field, only to have the engine go off tune and lose the race to Graham Hill. The World Championship was still undecided and Jim Clark, Graham Hill and John Surtees were all in the running for victory, so the Mexican race was of especial importance. Any hopes that Hill had of winning the Championship evaporated when his B.R.M. was rammed by Bandini's Ferrari and he was forced to stop for his damaged exhaust pipes to be cut away. Bandini then spun, allowing team-mate Surtees to move up into third place. In the closing stages of the race Clark's Lotus started to drop an oil trail and on the very last lap his engine seized up. So Gurney won the race for Brabham, and Surtees, with luck very much on his side, finished second and took the Drivers' Championship by the narrow margin of one point.

1965

Although Coventry-Climax had been planning a new and very advanced flat-16 engine for the 1965 season, this was never raced; the firm did, however, produce a new 32-valve version of the V-8 and this engine was used by Lotus and Brabham with great effect. For 1965 Honda had two cars ready to race, improved in a whole host of ways and driven by Richie Ginther and Bucknum. At Bourne Ginther's place was taken by the up and coming young driver Jackie Stewart who obviously had tremendous potential. In the Cooper team the number two driver was now young Austrian Jochen Rindt. Rob Walker had now taken Swiss privateer Jo Siffert and his Brabham under his wing and entered this car as well as his usual Brabham driven by Joakim Bonnier.

The South African race had been put back in the calendar so that it was no longer the last race of the 1964 season, but the first of 1965 and was held in January. Jim Clark, whose Lotus was still fitted with the 16-valve engine simply ran away from the opposition, and he scored what was to prove the first of six

6

16

(*Above, left*) 1964 World Champion John Surtees at the wheel of his flat-12 Ferrari in the 1965 Dutch race.

(*Right*) Graham Hill at the wheel of the final version of the V-8 1.5-litre B.R.M. in the 1965 British race at Silverstone.

victories out of six races entered. The B.R.M.s were on top form at Monaco and by the chequered flag, Hill had fought his way to the front and Stewart finished third. Clark's car had the 32-valve engine at Spa and on a wet track he was unchallenged, but young Stewart, driving for the first time on this very fast and very difficult circuit, took a fine second place.

The next round was the French race, held in 1965 on the superb Circuit d'Auvergne road circuit at Clermont-Ferrand. This swoops, ascends and twists its way through the countryside for 4.06 miles and it is essentially a driver's circuit. In the 1965 race Clark's driving skill was unchallenged, and second place went to Jackie Stewart. The British race reverted to Silverstone in 1965 and Clark won once again. At Zandvoort Ginther's Honda took the lead initially, but the American was soon passed by both Hill and Clark, Lotus went ahead of B.R.M., while Stewart repeated his Clermont form and passed his team-leader to finish second. Clark's victory at the Nürburgring was another resounding triumph of his superiority over the opposition.

Monza was the scene of a tremendous battle between Clark, Hill and Stewart with each of them leading by a narrow margin at different stages in the race. Near the end Clark's Lotus expired out on the circuit with electrical trouble and then Hill led from Stewart. But on the last lap but one Hill put a wheel on the gravel at the edge of the track, lost time, and Stewart went on to his first Championship race by a margin of just under four seconds. In the United States race Clark retired when in the lead and Hill scored his second victory of the season. Clark was fastest in practice for the Mexican race, but the pacemaker proved to be Ginther's Honda and this led throughout to win from Dan Gurney's Brabham.

(*Opposite, top*) The maestro of the $1\frac{1}{2}$-litre Formula, Jim Clark, completely dominated the 1965 French race at Clermont-Ferrand at the wheel of his Lotus 33.

(*Bottom*) Denis Hulme finished fifth in a works Brabham in the same race.

14
OWEN RACING ORG

CHAPTER FIVE

The Years of Power, 1966-70

1966

WITH his new car, Ferrari had reverted to his traditional V-12 engine layout and the 2989 cc (77×53.5 mm) four overhead camshaft engine developed a claimed 360 bhp at 10,000 rpm. This engine was mounted in a monocoque body/chassis structure consisting of riveted aluminium sheet wrapped round steel tubes with the cockpit sides forming boxes to house the rubber fuel tanks. Ferrari also raced in some events in 1966 the car that had been built for Surtees to run in the Tasman races, but which had never been used. This had one of the old Dino 246 2·4-litre engines of 1958–60 using fuel injection.

The Cooper team had built a new monocoque car for 1966 and this was powered by a Maserati V-12 2989 cc (70.4×64 mm) four overhead camshaft engine developing 360 bhp at 9500 rpm. Although the Cooper was to prove over-weight and under-powered, in early 1966 it seemed to be one of the best of the new designs and in addition to the works cars driven by Richie Ginther and Jochen Rindt, Rob Walker bought one for Jo Siffert to drive and Joakim Bonnier and Guy Ligier raced their own. Jack Brabham had originally declared that his team would not be competing in the new Formula because they lacked a suitable engine, but in fact he produced new cars based on the 1964–5 design and powered by the Australian Repco engine. This was a simple V-8 design with a single overhead camshaft per bank of cylinders and the very modest power output of 285 bhp at 8200 rpm. But whatever the Brabham lacked in power was more than compensated for by its low weight, excellent handling and reliability. The Brabham drivers were Jack himself and New Zealander Denis Hulme who had driven Brabhams in a few 1965 Grands Prix.

Jackie Stewart hard at work with the H-16 B.R.M. in the 1967 Belgian race.

Bruce McLaren was now running his own team, but his first Indianapolis Ford-powered Grand Prix car was doomed to failure. Another driver turned constructor was Californian Dan Gurney who formed the All American Racers Team to field his superb-looking blue and silver Eagle cars.

The first round that year was at Monaco where Surtees with the V-12 Ferrari led until rear axle trouble brought his run to an end and Stewart won with a 2-litre B.R.M. Weather is the factor that makes the Spa track so dangerous and although it was dry at the start of the 1966 race, when the drivers reached the far side of the circuit, it was pouring with rain and the road surface was perilously slippery. A total of seven cars went off the road and Hill stopped to release team-mate Stewart from the cockpit of his crashed B.R.M. At the end of that first lap Surtees was in the lead, while Rindt, who had experienced a succession of terrifying high-speed spins on the Masta straight, was climbing back through the field with his Cooper-Maserati. By the end of the second lap he was in third place and two laps later he took the lead from Surtees. Blinded by spray from Rindt's wheels, Surtees had more sense than try to re-pass the Austrian, but as the race drew to a close, the rain abated, and Surtees came through to score his first Championship victory since his accident in a sports-car race in 1965.

At Le Mans Surtees left the Ferrari team after a disagreement with team-manager Dragoni and his services were immediately acquired by Cooper. The British team had already signed up Chris Amon, for they had lost Ginther back to Honda now that the Japanese team was almost ready to re-enter racing. At Reims, Jack Brabham scored a popular victory. The British race was at Brands Hatch and the Brabham team took the first two places.

The Dutch race was the following weekend and Brabham and Hulme went ahead at the start, chased hard by Hill's B.R.M. and Clark's Lotus-Climax 2-litre. Clark's driving in this race was truly inspired; he passed Hill, moved up to second place when Hulme retired and then snatched the lead from

(*Left*) British Grand Prix, 1966: (*Top*) Peter Arundell in his works Lotus 33. (*Bottom*) Dan Gurney's Eagle, powered by a Climax engine.

(*Opposite*) Lorenzo Bandini and his V-8 Ferrari in practice for the 1965 British race.

(*Above*) Triple World Champion Jack Brabham on the starting grid at Brands Hatch.

(*Right*) Jack Brabham at the wheel of his Brabham-Repco in the 1966 German race which he won.

(*Above*) John Surtees, in his heavy Cooper-Maserati, took second place in the 1966 German race.

Brabham. At two-thirds race distance Clark's Lotus developed a water leak and after a stop to take on more water, he finished third, undoubtedly the moral victor, although beaten on the road by both Brabham and Hill. The German race was another event run in miserable, wet conditions and Brabham and Surtees were uncatchable. Once Surtees had left the Ferrari team, its fortunes had waned, but at Monza Scarfiotti driving on home territory led home Mike Parkes in a fine one-two finish and it was a victory that gave the team much encouragement.

Jim Clark drove the B.R.M. H-16-engined Lotus in the United States Grand Prix, to everyone's surprise this excessively complicated engine lasted the race distance and Clark scored a most improbable victory. Surtees might well have won this race, but for a collision with Peter Arundell's Lotus. To round off the season was the Mexican race and here Surtees derived some consolation for his Watkins Glen mishap and won the race from the Brabhams.

1967

Substantial changes were made to few of the cars for the 1967 season, but a number of drivers swapped stables. John Surtees signed up with Honda, while Ginther drove a second

(*Overleaf*) (*Left*) Jack Brabham at Silverstone in 1964. (*Right*) Jackie Stewart drove the MS 10 Matra-Cosworth brilliantly during the 1968 season and was only narrowly beaten into second place in the Drivers' Championship.

DUNLOP

FERODO
JACKIE STEWART

(*Above*) Jackie Stewart driving the heavy and complex H-16 B.R.M. in the 1967 Belgian race, in which he took second place. (*Below*) In the French Grand Prix at Le Mans, Chris Amon drove this V-12 Ferrari, but retired.

Eagle in some races, and Chris Amon, who had been given very few drives by Cooper, joined Ferrari. Jochen Rindt, now entering the last year of his three-year contract with Cooper, was joined by Pedro Rodriguez. After seven successive seasons with B.R.M., Graham Hill had rejoined Lotus, but it was made clear that he and Jim Clark were joint number one drivers and there was no team-leader as such. Stewart led the B.R.M. team, but he was joined by Mike Spence, a very steady and reliable driver who had not been very well treated at Lotus. During 1966 McLaren had resorted to using the Italian Serenissima V-8 engine as a substitute for the unsatisfactory Ford in a number of races, but he had now abandoned the original Grand Prix chassis. Instead he drove a Formula Two McLaren with B.R.M. 2-litre engine in some races and also handled on occasion a works Eagle.

The season opened with the South African race which was now held on the 2.5-mile Kyalami circuit near Johannesburg. Although it proved a victory by default, as one by one the leading cars dropped out, Rodriguez scored Cooper's second successive Championship race victory. An interesting race in

March was the Race of the Champions at Brands Hatch, held in two heats and a final and a form of try-out before the main European season got under way. This provided Gurney and the V-12 Eagle with a most encouraging victory and Surtees with the Honda took second place in one of the heats.

At Monaco Hulme scored a fine victory, but Bandini was the victim of one of the most horrible accidents that motor racing has ever seen. Monaco is a very tiring circuit that tests a driver's powers of concentration to the limit and on lap 82 a very weary Bandini hit the wooden barriers at the chicane, the car mounted the straw bales at the outside of the corner, overturned and burst into flames. The car was turned back on to its wheels by the marshalls, but then the fuel tank exploded and by the time the driver could be rescued from the inferno, he was terribly burnt and he succumbed to his injuries.

At the Dutch race almost a month later there appeared the long-awaited new Lotus 49 powered by the Ford-financed Cosworth engine. This brilliant piece of engineering was a V-8 of 2993 cc (85.7 × 64.8 mm), of all-aluminium construction and with a power output of 400 bhp at 9000 rpm. The chassis was of advanced concept to match the engine and from the moment it appeared it was clear that the 49 was the most formidable 3-litre car built so far. And the car did all that could possibly be expected of it at Zandvoort; Hill was fastest in practice and led the race until his engine failed, and then Clark moved up into the lead to score a resounding victory, over half a minute ahead of the second place Brabham.

At Spa Gurney scored the Eagle's one and only Championship victory, as well as setting a new lap record of 148.85 mph.

(*Overleaf*) During 1969 Jacky Ickx drove a works Brabham and took second place in the Drivers' Championship.

Sole Championship victory for Dan Gurney and the Eagle came in the 1967 Belgian race at Spa. The very fast American V-12 cars were plagued by engine troubles which were never completely overcome.

(*Above*) British Grand Prix, 1967: (*Left*) Jim Clark in the new Lotus 49 with Ford-Cosworth engine. (*Right*) The ex-works 1966 Brabham driven by Guy Ligier.

(*Below*) 1967 World Champion Denis Hulme who won the Monaco and German races at the wheel of Brabham.

In this race Mike Parkes had a nasty crash with his works Ferrari and for the rest of the season Chris Amon alone represented Maranello.

In 1967 the French Grand Prix was held at Le Mans. Both of the Lotus 49s retired with final drive failure and the works Brabhams took the first two places. At Silverstone the Lotus 49s dominated the race until Hill's retirement and then Clark scored the model's second victory with Hulme's Brabham in second place. At the Nürburgring there was no holding the partnership of Hulme and Brabham and these drivers once again took the first two places.

An addition to the Championship calendar in 1967 was the Canadian Grand Prix which was ruined by torrential rain. In an almost monotonous repetition of earlier races, Clark built up an unassailable lead with his Lotus 49 only to retire – this time because of wet electrics – and Brabham and Hulme took the first two places. Hill in this race never succeeded in mastering the adverse conditions and finished fourth.

At Monza Honda produced a new car with a much improved chassis designed and built in the Lola works. Clark built up a good lead in the opening laps of the race, but was forced to stop at the pits because of a puncture. He rejoined the race to take the lead from team-mate Hill. Hill's car broke its engine and just when it seemed as though Lotus had this race in the bag, Clark's engine started to mis-fire because of a fault in the fuel pick-up system. Surtees with the new Honda and Brabham swept by the stricken Lotus and at the finish the Japanese car led the green and the gold of the Brabham by a matter of feet. By the United States race, Team Lotus had found reliability to match the speed of their cars and Clark and Hill came home in the first two places – and this was a victory repeated by Clark at Mexico City. The real kudos in 1967, however, went to the Brabham team, for Hulme, following in his team-leader's wheel-tracks, won the 1967 Drivers' Championship through consistency and persistency and Brabham was second, only five points behind.

1968

For the 1968 season Lotus drivers remained unchanged and after the South African race the cars ran in the red, white and gold colours of Player's Gold Leaf from which they were receiving sponsorship. When Jim Clark was so tragically killed in a Formula Two race at Hockenheim, his place was taken by Jackie Oliver. Rob Walker acquired a Lotus 49 for Jo Siffert to drive. B.R.M. abandoned the disastrously unsuccessful H-16 cars and raced instead simpler and lighter cars powered by the V-12 engine that had first been seen in McLaren's car at Mosport in 1967. The team drivers were Mike Spence and Pedro Rodriguez, but when Spence was killed while qualifying at Indianapolis with a Lotus, Dickie Attwood was brought into the team.

Ford had decided to make the 3-litre Grand Prix engine available to everyone and the McLaren team produced at the Race of the Champions their new Cosworth-powered M7A car. Bruce McLaren had been joined by Denis Hulme and they made a steady, restrained and well-balanced combination. At Brabham, Hulme's place was taken by Jochen Rindt. Another user of the Cosworth engine was the new Matra International team which was formed by Ken Tyrrell to race the French Matra MS10 chassis. Chris Amon was joined at Ferrari by young Belgian Jacky Ickx who was entering Grand Prix racing after a sensational career with Formula Two Matras.

Team Lotus dominated the South African race with Clark and Hill coming home in the first two places, but the Matra-Cosworth driven by Stewart ran well before retiring with engine failure and it was clearly a car of great potential. Unfortunately Stewart injured his wrist in a Formula Two race at Madrid in April and was unable to race again until the Belgian Grand Prix in June. After an interval of fourteen years the Spanish race had been restored to the series, but it was now held on an artificial circuit at Madrid. Here the Brabham team unveiled

(*Above*) The Matra International Cosworth-powered MS10 car raced by Jackie Stewart during 1968.

(*Overleaf*) (*Left*) The four-wheel-drive Matra MS 84 seen in practice at Silverstone in 1969, with Jackie Stewart at the wheel. (*Right*) Jackie Ickx in the Belgian Grand Prix, driving the fastest car raced during 1970, the new Ferrari 312 B.

30
MATRA

27

Graham Hill at the wheel of the works Lotus which he drove to victory in the 1968 Monaco Grand Prix.

their latest BT26 model with aluminium sheeting riveted to the chassis tubes to stiffen the chassis and the new Repco four-cam engine. There were only five finishers in this race, Hill's works Lotus leading home Hulme, the Coopers of Redman and Scarfiotti and Beltoise bringing up the rear with the Tyrrell Matra. At Monaco Graham Hill, who so far in the season had faced little in the way of serious opposition, scored his second consecutive victory.

An innovation at the Belgian race was the use by Brabham and Ferrari of a rear-mounted aerofoil and this was a fashion to which all the Grand Prix constructors were to become addicted. Stewart drove a magnificent race with his Matra, but due to a miscalculation he ran out of fuel when leading and a pit stop at the end of the last lap but one dropped him to fourth place. So the winner was Bruce McLaren, enjoying the taste of a Grand Prix victory for the first time since his win with a Cooper at Reims in 1962.

As the season progressed, so the opposition to Lotus increased in strength. At Zandvoort, Stewart achieved a fine victory with the Matra which was now a match for its Gold Leaf rivals and Beltoise with the V-12 car did unexpectedly well to finish second. Honda entered their new air-cooled RA302 car for Frenchman Jo Schlesser to drive at Rouen, but he was killed when the car crashed, overturned and became a burning holocaust of petrol and magnesium. The French race brought a first World Championship victory for Jacky Ickx, and Ferraris took second and third places in the British race at Brands Hatch. The winner on the Kent circuit was Jo Siffert with Rob Walker's private Lotus who inherited the lead after the retirement of the works 49s and this was the first Championship race win by a private owner since Moss's victory for Walker at the Nürburgring in 1961. The German race was held in the worst possible conditions, heavy rain that made the circuit awash and yet, at the same time, a thick veil of mist which in places reduced visibility to a few yards. In these conditions there was only one driver who could be described as racing and that was Jackie Stewart who displayed tremendous skill and at the finish led by over four minutes from Hill's Lotus. As usual, the last European round was at Monza where Hulme scored a win for McLaren, while Servoz-Gavin with a second Tyrrell Matra just pipped Ickx' Ferrari for second place.

In practice for the Canadian race, Ickx crashed his Ferrari and was lucky to escape with a broken leg. Both Hill and Stewart made pit stops in this race and so Hulme and McLaren took the first two places in a manner reminiscent of the Brabham performances of the previous year. At the United States race, Indianapolis driver Mario Andretti was at the wheel of a works Lotus and he took to Grand Prix driving at once, handling his car in a stylish, beautifully controlled manner, but what is more he astounded the usual Grand Prix

(*Below, left*) On the rain-soaked Nürburgring, Jackie Stewart scored a brilliant victory with his Matra in the 1968 German Grand Prix. (*Below, right*) Jackie Ickx and his V-12 Ferrari finished third in the 1968 British Grand Prix.

Shell
GOODYEAR
18
FERODO
FERODO

'set' by making fastest time in practice and holding second place in the race until forced to make a pit stop for attention to the body of the Lotus. Stewart who had been the one man in front of Andretti won the race with Hill second. At Mexico City Stewart was in second place behind Hill when the Matra's handling deteriorated because of a cracked chassis and he fell back to finish fourth. Hill won his second World Championship by a margin of twelve points.

(*Above*) John Surtees in action with the 1968 version of the V-12 Honda.

(*Opposite*) Promising newcomer to Grand Prix racing in 1970 was Ronnie Peterson who raced this March 701 in the French Grand Prix at Clermont-Ferrand.

1969

With the withdrawal of Eagle, Honda and Cooper at the end of the 1968 season, racing became completely dominated by the Ford-Cosworth engine, especially as Brabham now used it in their existing chassis to replace the totally unsuccessful four-cam Repco and the Matra works team had withdrawn from the Grand Prix scene to concentrate on sports car racing. Jacky Ickx left Ferrari to join Brabham, while Rindt moved on to the Lotus team where for most of the season he and Hill behaved as if they were deadly rivals and not team-mates. Like several other constructors Lotus produced a four-wheel-drive car and this was in the main driven by newcomer John Miles. Matra had entrusted their entire Grand Prix programme to Ken Tyrrell who fielded the new Cosworth-powered MS80 cars for Stewart and Jean-Pierre Beltoise. There was also a four-wheel-drive Matra, the MS84, and although this ran in a few races it was purely experimental. There were no changes at McLaren, although this team too had built a four-wheel-drive model, the M9A, which appeared only at the British race, with Derek Bell at the wheel. Ferrari soldiered on with his V-12 cars driven by Chris Amon and also in a couple of races by Pedro Rodriguez, but they were now outclassed. Equally hopeless

(*Below*) Fast and furious in 1969 was the driving of Jochen Rindt at the wheel of his works Lotus 49 B.

was the position at Bourne, for during the 1969 season the V-12 B.R.M.s were uncompetitive and unreliable and the team's two new drivers, John Surtees and Jackie Oliver, had a completely miserable season of failure after failure.

The season was completely dominated by the skill of Jackie Stewart and the speed and good handling of the Matra. Nevertheless, Ickx at the wheel of his Brabham combined courage with good sense and won two races. It is significant that of the eleven Championship races Stewart made fastest lap at five (as well as winning six), Ickx at three (in the Canadian race he shared fastest lap with Brabham) and Rindt at two. Stewart won the South African race with the old MS10 car, but then switched to the MS80. The 1969 Spanish Grand Prix was held in Montjuich Park, Barcelona, a fine road circuit. Rindt took the lead at the start, but both Hill in second place and the Austrian crashed badly when their aerofoils broke at high speed, and Stewart scored another victory. Because of anxieties about the safety of aerofoils, these were suddenly banned after the first practice session at Monaco and the cars had to run in the race 'naked'. Unexpectedly the two Matras retired with drive-shaft failure when in first and second places and Graham Hill scored his fifth victory in the race. By Zandvoort the F.I.A. had relented and small aerofoils forming part of the bodywork were allowed. The opening laps of the Dutch race were fought out between the two works Lotus 49s which bumped and bored into each other round the circuit until Rindt broke away and seared into the distance. Stewart slipped ahead of Hill and then assumed the lead when the leading Lotus retired.

The Belgian race was cancelled in 1969 and so the next round was at Clermont-Ferrand. The undulations of the circuit made Rindt feel ill, Hill was never at his best at Clermont and so there were only three drivers in the race. While Stewart motored away into the distance, his team-mate Beltoise, who knows Clermont intimately, battled with Ickx and snatched second place away from him on the very last lap, much to the delight of the French crowd. Jack Brabham missed this, the British and the German races because of a testing accident. The British race resolved itself into a duel between Rindt and Stewart, with first the Austrian leading, then Stewart, then Rindt again. But this came to an end when Rindt's aerofoil broke and he came into the pits for it to be torn off. Although

(*Left, top*) World Champion-to-be Jackie Stewart took first place in the 1969 British Grand Prix in his Matra MS80-Cosworth.

(*Left, bottom*) Jackie Ickx in his Brabham BT26 was second in the same race.

(*Below*) Jean-Pierre Beltoise finished fifth in the 1970 Dutch race at the wheel of the V-12 Matra MS120.

(*Right*) Denis Hulme at Monaco in 1969 with his McLaren-Cosworth.

Rindt rejoined the race without losing second place, a fuel stop caused him to drop back, Ickx moved into second spot, but he coasted across the finishing line with a dead engine after running out of fuel on the last lap.

At the Nürburgring, Ickx at the peak of his form out-drove Stewart, who fell back in the later stages of the race with gearbox trouble. The Belgian was unable to repeat this performance at Monza because of an early pit stop caused by an oil leak. The Italian race was memorable for the furiously close racing between a tight bunch of cars that lasted for the whole 68 laps, and at the start of the 68th any one of four cars could still have won. Stewart crossed the line less than a tenth of a second ahead of Rindt and Beltoise was right behind the Lotus. Just as Clark had scored a whole run of wins in 1965 and then had his luck run out, so Stewart gained no further success in 1969. What should have been a great race became a walkover for Ickx when he and Stewart collided in the Canadian Grand Prix. Rindt scored his first Championship victory at Watkins Glen after Stewart had retired with an oil leak and Hulme was the well-deserving winner at Mexico City after a season of restrained and careful driving.

1970

At the 1969 Italian race there had appeared in practice the new Ferrari 312B car with horizontally-opposed 12-cylinder engine, and Jacky Ickx returned to the Ferrari team to drive this new and very promising car. His team-mates were Clay Regazzoni, an Italian-speaking Swiss and Ignazio Giunti, who had previously driven sports cars for the Autodelta team. Matra had returned to racing with the new and very much improved

(*Above*) In 1970 the Yardley perfume company sponsored the B.R.M. team. Jackie Oliver is seen at the British Grand Prix.

(*Below*) Jackie Stewart on his way to victory with the March 701 in the 1970 Spanish Grand Prix at Jarama.

MS120 model to be driven by Beltoise and Henri Pescarolo. There were now to be no Ford-powered Matras, and so Ken Tyrrell had to find a new mount for the World Champion. He chose the March car made by a British concern based at Bicester, whose cars were designed by Robin Herd. As number two in his team Tyrrell chose Johnny Servoz-Gavin, but when he retired from racing in mid-season his place was taken by another young Frenchman, Francois Cevert.

The works Marches were handled by Chris Amon and Jo Siffert. In some races Mario Andretti drove a March entered by the S.T.P. concern. A fourth car was entered for young Swedish driver Ronnie Peterson by Colin Crabbe. Both Brabham and McLaren had built new cars for the coming season. The McLaren was the M14A and in addition to the cars raced by the usual drivers, another with Alfa Romeo engine was fielded for Andrea de Adamich. Brabham himself was the sole works representative at the wheel of his new BT33 car, but a second car, driven by Rolf Stommelen, was entered by the German magazine *Auto Motor und Sport*.

Lotus produced the brilliant new 72 model, but while this was being developed drivers Rindt and Miles had to make do with the old cars, now in modified 49C form. Graham Hill had left the works team and drove a private Lotus for Rob Walker. The B.R.M. team was now receiving backing from the Yardley perfume company and the new P153 cars were painted in Yardley brown, white and gold colours and distinguished by a large 'Y' on the nose. Apart from the regular entries for drivers Rodriguez and Oliver, a third car was entered for Canadian George Eaton at most races. John Surtees was running an ex-works McLaren, but was also working hard to get his own TS7 Cosworth-powered car ready and this finally made its race debut in the British Grand Prix. With ten different teams competing, Grand Prix racing could hardly have been in a healthier state.

Now 44 years of age, Brabham displayed undiminished skill and speed during the 1970 season and, but for the most atrocious luck, would have won three races. As it was, he scored a fine victory in the first Championship round at Kyalami, while Stewart with the March not only won the Race of the Champions at Brands Hatch, but scored a very convincing victory at Madrid. So it seemed at this early stage in the season that racing was to witness yet another Jackie Stewart year. As events turned out, the new Lotus and the Ferrari were to prove faster and handle infinitely better than any of the opposition and Stewart was to have a most unsatisfactory season. The Monaco race should have proved Brabham's second victory of the season, but on the last corner of the last lap he left his braking late and as the turquoise BT33 crunched into the barriers, Rindt with the old Lotus 49C swept past to victory. Brabham rejoined the race to take second place.

Bruce McLaren lost his life in a testing crash with a McLaren Can-Am car and as a result the McLaren team did not run in the Belgian race. Here Pedro Rodriguez gladdened the heart of all B.R.M. enthusiasts who had seen the team sink to an all-time low and with the new P153 he scored a fine victory ahead of Amon's March. Another tragedy marred the Grand Prix year when Piers Courage crashed his Italian de Tomaso car at Zandvoort and perished in the ensuing inferno. The race brought Lotus their first victory with the new 72 and the first of four in succession for both car and Rindt, but the tragic accident made it a very unhappy occasion for everyone. Ickx led the French race at Clermont-Ferrand until his engine broke and then Beltoise took the lead with the angular Matra only to fall out of the running when a tyre punctured. If Rindt's victory was by default here, it was even more so in the British race where Brabham took the lead only to run out of fuel on the last lap and he was passed as he coasted towards the finishing line. Because the organisers had not carried out promised safety improvements at the Nürburgring, the drivers refused to compete there and the race was switched to the Hockenheim circuit near Heidelberg. Here Rindt had to fight with Ickx' Ferrari for his victory, but as the Belgian admitted after the race the Lotus was faster than the Ferrari – a situation that was soon to change.

A new circuit, the Österreichring, had been built near the site of the old Zeltweg circuit and here was held the first Championship Austrian Grand Prix since the 1964 race. On this circuit composed of a succession of fast curves, the Ferraris came into their own and Ickx and Regazzoni took the first two places. What was all the more remarkable was that Regazzoni's first ever Grand Prix had been the British race a few weeks earlier. At Monza Regazzoni scored a brilliant victory with Stewart tagging home in second place after one of the most

Jack Brabham at Clermont-Ferrand in 1970. He lost the race through a minor accident on the last lap.

enervating drives of his career. But the delight of the very patriotic Italian crowd was completely overshadowed by the terrible tragedy in practice. For no known reason Rindt's Lotus had crashed into the barriers lining the track and the Austrian Champion-to-be who had been considering retirement at the end of the season was fatally injured.

Used in practice at Monza, but not raced, was the new Tyrrell car which the team had built themselves. This car, incorporating some of the design features of old Matra MS80, was driven by Stewart in the Canadian race. He led the field with ease until a stub axle broke and Ferraris again took the first two places. It was to be much the same story at Watkins Glen where Stewart retired with engine trouble. Here Rodriguez took the lead with his B.R.M., but dropped to third place after an unscheduled fuel stop. The winner was brilliant new recruit to the Lotus team, Brazilian Emerson Fittipaldi and in third place came another new Lotus driver, Swedish Reine Wisell. Lack of crowd control almost caused the cancellation of the Mexican race where Ferraris yet again took the first two places.

The 1970 season had seen Grand Prix racing at its best, in terms of technical diversity and development, closeness of racing and in the large number of starters in each race. But it was also one of the most tragic years and the sport suffered the loss of three of its greatest personalities. There could be no greater indication of the perils that accompany this exacting and exciting sport than the fact that the 1970 Drivers' Championship was a posthumous award.

(*Above*) Winner at Zandvoort was 1970 World Champion Jochen Rindt at the wheel of the new and brilliantly successful Lotus 72.

(*Below*) Denis Hulme driving his new McLaren M 14A at Monaco in 1970.

Appendix

GRAND PRIX RACING FORMULAE

1947–51: Maximum engine capacities of 1500 cc supercharged and 4500 cc unsupercharged. The smaller capacity was that of pre-war 'Voiturettes', the then equivalent of the Formula Two category, and the larger capacity was the alternative to the 3000 cc supercharged Formula of the years 1938–46.

1952–3: Although the above Formula officially remained in force until the end of the 1953 season, during these years all World Championship races were held to Formula Two rules, that is with maximum engine capacities of 2000 cc unsupercharged and 500 cc supercharged. The smaller size was technically impractical and no cars of this engine size were raced.

1954–60: Maximum engine capacities of 2500 cc unsupercharged and 750 cc supercharged. Again, the smaller capacity was impractical and had been allowed because the B.R.M. team had expressed an interest in building engines of this size based on one half of their existing V-16 1500 cc unit. The only cars with 750 cc engines to be raced were French D.B.-Panhard cars which ran in a few minor races. From 1958 the use of 'Avgas' (100/130 octane aviation fuel) was compulsory.

1961–5: Minimum engine capacity of 1301 cc and maximum capacity of 1500 cc unsupercharged. Minimum dry weight of 450 kg. Commercial fuel was compulsory and all cars had to be fitted with self-starters. No replenishment of oil during a race was allowed for reasons of safety. This Formula was similar to the Formula Two that had been in force between 1957 and 1960, but the requirement relating to self-starters was new.

1966–70: Maximum capacities of 3000 cc unsupercharged and 1500 cc supercharged. Other regulations as for 1961–5.

MINIMUM RACE DISTANCES FOR GRANDS PRIX

1950–7: 300 km *or* three hours.

1958–65: Between 300 and 500 km *and* two hours.

1966–70: Between 300 and 400 km.

These minimum distances have not always been strictly adhered to.

RULES GOVERNING THE DRIVERS' AND MANUFACTURERS' WORLD CHAMPIONSHIPS

DRIVERS' WORLD CHAMPIONSHIP

The Championship is awarded on the basis of points gained in the specified major events. Up to and including 1959, eight, six, four, three and two points respectively were awarded for the first five places, together with one point for fastest lap in the race. In 1960 the point for fastest lap was dropped and one point given for sixth place. In 1961 the winner's points were increased from eight to nine. Up until 1957, where more than one driver shared a car, they shared the points, but from 1958 onwards points were awarded only to a driver who handled the car throughout the race. A driver can only count a specified number of Championship rounds towards his personal total.

QUALIFYING ROUNDS IN THE DRIVERS' WORLD CHAMPIONSHIP

Argentine Grand Prix, 1953–8, 1960
Austrian Grand Prix, 1964, 1970
Belgian Grand Prix, 1950–6, 1958, 1960–8, 1970
British Grand Prix, 1950–70
Canadian Grand Prix, 1967–70
Dutch Grand Prix, 1952–3, 1955, 1958–70
French Grand Prix, 1950–4, 1956–70
German Grand Prix, 1951–4, 1956–9, 1961–70
Indianapolis 500 Miles race, 1950–60
Italian Grand Prix, 1950–70
Mexican Grand Prix, 1963–70
Monaco Grand Prix, 1950, 1955–70
Moroccan Grand Prix, 1958
Pescara Grand Prix, 1957
Portuguese Grand Prix, 1958–60
South African Grand Prix, 1962–5, 1967–70
Spanish Grand Prix, 1951, 1954, 1968–70
Swiss Grand Prix, 1950–4
United States Grand Prix, 1959–70

TOTAL OF QUALIFYING EVENTS

	Total events held	Total that a driver could count towards his final score
1950	7	4
1951	8	4
1952	8	4
1953	9	4
1954	9	5
1955	7	5
1956	8	5
1957	8	5
1958	11	6
1959	9	5
1960	10	6
1961	8	5
1962	9	5
1963	10	6
1964	10	6
1965	10	6
1966	9	5
1967	11	*
1968	12	*
1969	12	*
1970	13	*

* Since 1967 the season has been divided into two equal sections. If there is an uneven number of qualifying events, the first section will contain one more event than the second section. Drivers may count the points obtained from all but one of the races in each section towards their final score.

MANUFACTURERS' WORLD CHAMPIONSHIP

Although a World Championship of Manufacturers had been held during the years, 1925–7, the present Championship was not introduced until the 1958 season. The Championship is awarded on a points system on the results of the races in the Drivers' Championship. Originally eight, six, four, three and two points were awarded for the first five places, but one point for sixth place was added in 1960. The points for the winning car were increased from eight to nine in 1962. The same total number of events may be counted as in the Drivers' Championship and only the highest placed of each make is awarded points.

RACE RESULTS, 1950–70

1950:

European Grand Prix, Silverstone (202 miles), 13 May
1st, G.Farina (Alfa Romeo 158), 90.95 mph; 2nd, L.Fagioli (Alfa Romeo 158); 3rd, R.Parnell (Alfa Romeo 158).

Monaco Grand Prix, Monte Carlo (195 miles), 21 May
1st, J.M.Fangio (Alfa Romeo 158), 61.33 mph; 2nd, A. Ascari (Ferrari Tipo 125); 3rd, L. Chiron (Maserati 4CLT/48).

Swiss Grand Prix, Bremgarten (190 miles), 4 June
1st,. G.Farina (Alfa Romeo 158), 92.76 mph; 2nd, L.Fagioli (Alfa Romeo 158); 3rd, L. Rosier (Lago-Talbot).

Belgian Grand Prix, Spa-Francorchamps (306 miles), 18 June
1st, J.M.Fangio (Alfa Romeo 158), 109.98 mph; 2nd, L.Fagioli (Alfa Romeo 158), 3rd, L.Rosier (Lago-Talbot).

French Grand Prix, Reims (310 miles), 2 July
1st, J.M.Fangio (Alfa Romeo 158), 104.83 mph; 2nd, L.Fagioli (Alfa Romeo 158); 3rd, P.N.Whitehead (Ferrari Tipo 125).

Italian Grand Prix, Monza (313 miles), 3 September
1st, G. Farina (Alfa Romeo 159), 109.63 mph; 2nd, D. Serafini/A.Ascari (Ferrari Tipo 375); 3rd, L.Fagioli (Alfa Romeo 158).

Drivers' World Championship:
1st, G.Farina (30 points); 2nd, J.M.Fangio (27 points); 3rd, L.Fagioli (24 points).

1951:

Swiss Grand Prix, Bremgarten (190 miles), 27 May
1st J.M.Fangio (Alfa Romeo 159), 89.18 mph; 2nd, P.Taruffi (Ferrari Tipo 375); 3rd, G.Farina (Alfa Romeo 159).

Belgian Grand Prix, Spa-Francorchamps (315 miles), 17 June
1st, G.Farina (Alfa Romeo 159), 114.32 mph; 2nd, A.Ascari (Ferrari Tipo 375); 3rd, L.Villoresi (Ferrari Tipo 375).

European Grand Prix, Reims (374 miles), 1 July
1st, J.M.Fangio (Alfa Romeo 159), 110.97 mph; 2nd, J.F. Gonzalez/A.Ascari (Ferrari Tipo 375); 3rd, L.Villoresi (Ferrari Tipo 375).

British Grand Prix, Silverstone (260 miles), 14 July
1st, J.F.Gonzalez (Ferrari Tipo 375), 96.11 mph; 2nd, J.M. Fangio (Alfa Romeo 159); 3rd, L. Villoresi (Ferrari Tipo 375).

German Grand Prix, Nürburgring (283 miles), 29 July
1st, A.Ascari (Ferrari Tipo 375), 83.76 mph; 2nd, J.M.Fangio (Alfa Romeo 159); 3rd, J.F. Gonzalez (Ferrari Tipo 375).

Italian Grand Prix, Monza (313 miles), 16 September
1st, A.Ascari (Ferrari Tipo 375), 115.52 mph; 2nd, J.F.Gonzalez (Ferrari Tipo 375); 3rd, F.Bonetto/G.Farina (Alfa Romeo 159M).

Spanish Grand Prix, Pedralbes (275 miles), 20 October
1st, J.M.Fangio (Alfa Romeo 159M), 98.76 mph; 2nd, J.F. Gonzalez (Ferrari Tipo 375); 3rd, G. Farina (Alfa Romeo 159M).

Drivers' World Championship:
1st, J.M.Fangio (31 points); 2nd, A.Ascari (25 points); 3rd, J.F.Gonzalez (24 points).

1952:

Swiss Grand Prix, Bremgarten (280 miles), 18 May
1st, P.Taruffi (Ferrari Tipo 500), 92.60 mph; 2nd, R.Fischer (Ferrari Tipo 500); 3rd, J.Behra (Gordini).

European Grand Prix, Spa-Francorchamps (315 miles), 22 June
1st, A.Ascari (Ferrari Tipo 500), 102.90 mph; 2nd, G.Farina (Ferrari Tipo 500); 3rd, R.Manzon (Gordini).

French Grand Prix, Rouen-les-Essarts (three hours), 6 July
1st, A.Ascari (Ferrari Tipo 500), 80.08 mph (240.39 miles); 2nd, G.Farina (Ferrari Tipo 500); 3rd, P.Taruffi (Ferrari Tipo 500).

British Grand Prix, Silverstone (249 miles), 19 July
1st, A.Ascari (Ferrari Tipo 500), 90.92 mph; 2nd, P.Taruffi (Ferrari Tipo 500); 3rd, J.M.Hawthorn (Cooper-Bristol).

German Grand Prix, Nürburgring (255 miles), 3 August
1st, A.Ascari (Ferrari Tipo 500), 82.09 mph; 2nd, G.Farina (Ferrari Tipo 500); 3rd, R.Fischer (Ferrari Tipo 500).

Dutch Grand Prix, Zandvoort (234 miles), 17 August
1st, A.Ascari (Ferrari Tipo 500), 80.95 mph; 2nd, G.Farina (Ferrari Tipo 500); 3rd, L.Villoresi (Ferrari Tipo 500).

Italian Grand Prix, Monza (313 miles), 7 September
1st, A.Ascari (Ferrari Tipo 500), 109.80 mph; 2nd, J.F.Gonzalez (Maserati A6GCM); 3rd, L.Villoresi (Ferrari Tipo 500).

Drivers' World Championship:
1st, A.Ascari (36 points); 2nd, G.Farina (24 points); 3rd, P. Taruffi (22 points).

1953:

Argentine Grand Prix, Buenos Aires (252 miles), 18 January
1st, A.Ascari (Ferrari Tipo 500), 78.12 mph; 2nd, L.Villoresi (Ferrari Tipo 500); 3rd, J.F.Gonzalez (Maserati A6GCM).

Dutch Grand Prix, Zandvoort (235 miles), 7 June
1st, A.Ascari (Ferrari Tipo 500), 81.04 mph; 2nd, G.Farina (Ferrari Tipo 500); 3rd, F.Bonetto/J.F.Gonzalez (Maserati A6SSG).

Belgian Grand Prix, Spa-Francorchamps (315 miles), 21 June
1st, A.Ascari (Ferrari Tipo 500), 112.47 mph; 2nd, L.Villoresi (Ferrari Tipo 500); 3rd, O.Marimon (Maserati A6SSG).

French Grand Prix, Reims (312 miles), 5 July
1st, J.M.Hawthorn (Ferrari Tipo 500), 113.65 mph; 2nd, J.M. Fangio (Maserati A6SSG); 3rd, J.F.Gonzalez (Maserati A6SSG).

British Grand Prix, Silverstone (263 miles), 18 July
1st, A.Ascari (Ferrari Tipo 500), 92.97 mph; 2nd, J.M.Fangio (Maserati A6SSG); 3rd, G.Farina (Ferrari Tipo 500).

German Grand Prix, Nürburgring (256 miles), 2 August
1st, G.Farina (Ferrari Tipo 500), 83.89 mph; 2nd, J.M.Fangio (Maserati A6SSG); 3rd, J.M.Hawthorn (Ferrari Tipo 500).

Swiss Grand Prix, Bremgarten (294 miles), 23 August
1st, A.Ascari (Ferrari Tipo 500), 97.17 mph; 2nd, G.Farina (Ferrari Tipo 500); 3rd, J.M.Hawthorn (Ferrari Tipo 500).

Italian Grand Prix, Monza (312 miles), 13 September
1st, J.M.Fangio (Maserati A6SSG), 110.69 mph; 2nd, G.Farina (Ferrari Tipo 500); 3rd, L.Villoresi (Ferrari Tipo 500).

Drivers' World Championship
1st, A.Ascari (34½ points); 2nd, J.M.Fangio (28 points); 3rd, G.Farina (26 points).

1954:

Argentine Grand Prix, Buenos Aires (three hours), 17 January
1st, J.M.Fangio (Maserati 250F), 70.13 mph; 2nd, G.Farina (Ferrari Tipo 625); 3rd, J.F.Gonzalez (Ferrari Tipo 625).

Belgian Grand Prix, Spa-Francorchamps (315 miles), 20 June
1st, J.M.Fangio (Maserati 250F), 115.08 mph; 2nd, M. Trintignant (Ferrari Tipo 625); 3rd, S.Moss (Maserati 250F).

French Grand Prix, Reims (312 miles), 4 July
1st, J.M.Fangio (Mercedes-Benz W.196), 115.67 mph; 2nd, K.Kling (Mercedes-Benz W.196); 3rd, R.Manzon (Ferrari Tipo 625).

British Grand Prix, Silverstone (270 miles), 17 July
1st, J.F.Gonzalez (Ferrari Tipo 625), 89.69 mph; 2nd, J.M. Hawthorn (Ferrari Tipo 625); 3rd, O.Marimon (Maserati).

European Grand Prix, Nürburgring (312 miles), 1 August
1st, J.M.Fangio (Mercedes-Benz W. 196), 82.77 mph; 2nd. J.F.Gonzalez/J.M.Hawthorn (Ferrari Tipo 625); 3rd, M. Trintignant (Ferrari Tipo 625).

Swiss Grand Prix, Bremgarten (280 miles), 22 August
1st, J.M.Fangio (Mercedes-Benz W.196), 99.17 mph; 2nd, J.F. Gonzalez (Ferrari Tipo 625); 3rd, H. Herrmann (Mercedes-Benz W.196).

Italian Grand Prix, Monza (313 miles), 5 September
1st, J.M.Fangio (Mercedes-Benz W. 196), 99.17 mph; 2nd, J.M.Hawthorn (Ferrari Tipo 625); 3rd, U.Maglioli/J.F. Gonzalez (Ferrari Tipo 625).

Spanish Grand Prix, Pedralbes (313 miles), 24 October
1st, J.M.Hawthorn (Ferrari Tipo 553), 97.93 mph; 2nd, L. Musso (Maserati 250F); 3rd, J.M.Fangio (Mercedes-Benz W.196).

Drivers' World Championship:
1st, J.M.Fangio (40 points); 2nd, J.F.Gonzalez ($25\frac{1}{7}$ points*); 3rd, J.M.Hawthorn ($24\frac{9}{14}$ points*).

* These fractions arose because of drivers sharing the point for fastest lap at certain races.

1955:

Argentine Grand Prix, Buenos Aires (three hours), 16 January
1st, J.M.Fangio (Mercedes-Benz W.196), 77.51 mph; 2nd, J.F. Gonzalez/G.Farina/M.Trintignant (Ferrari Tipo 625); 3rd, G. Farina/U.Maglioli/M.Trintignant (Ferrari Tipo 625).

European Grand Prix, Monaco (195 miles), 22 May
1st, M.Trintignant (Ferrari Tipo 625), 65.81 mph; 2nd, E. Castellotti (Lancia D.50); 3rd, C.Perdisa/J.Behra (Maserati 250F).

Belgian Grand Prix, Spa-Francorchamps (315 miles), 5 June
1st, J.M.Fangio (Mercedes-Benz W.196), 118.84 mph; 2nd, S.Moss (Mercedes-Benz W.196); 3rd, G.Farina (Ferrari Tipo 555).

Dutch Grand Prix. Zandvoort (260 miles), 19 June
1st, J.M.Fangio (Mercedes-Benz W.196), 89.62 mph; 2nd, S. Moss (Mercedes-Benz W.196); 3rd, L. Musso (Maserati 250F).

British Grand Prix, Aintree (270 miles), 16 July
1st, S.Moss (Mercedes-Benz W.196), 86.47 mph; 2nd, J.M. Fangio (Mercedes-Benz W.196); 3rd, K.Kling (Mercedes-Benz W. 196).

Italian Grand Prix, Monza (312 miles), 11 September
1st, J.M.Fangio (Mercedes-Benz W.196), 128.42 mph; 2nd, P.Taruffi (Mercedes-Benz W.196); 3rd, E.Castellotti (Ferrari Tipo 555).

Drivers' World Championship:
1st, J.M.Fangio (40 points); 2nd, S.Moss (23 points); 3rd, E.Castellotti (12 points).

1956:

Argentine Grand Prix, Buenos Aires (three hours), 22 January
1st, L.Musso/J.M.Fangio (Lancia-Ferrari), 79.38 mph; 2nd, J.Behra (Maserati 250F); 3rd, J.M.Hawthorn (Maserati 250F entered by the Owen Organisation).

Monaco Grand Prix, Monte Carlo (195 miles), 13 May
1st, S.Moss (Maserati 250F), 64.94 mph; 2nd, P.J.Collins/J.M. Fangio (Lancia-Ferrari); 3rd, J.Behra (Maserati 250F).

Belgian Grand Prix, Spa-Francorchamps (315 miles), 3 June
1st, P.J.Collins (Lancia-Ferrari), 118.43 mph; 2nd, P. Frère (Lancia-Ferrari); 3rd, C.Perdisa/S.Moss (Maserati 250F).

French Grand Prix, Reims (305 miles), 1 July
1st, P.J.Collins (Lancia-Ferrari), 122.21 mph; 2nd, E.Castellotti (Lancia-Ferrari); 3rd, J. Behra (Maserati 250F).

British Grand Prix, Silverstone (303 miles), 14 July
1st, J.M.Fangio (Lancia-Ferrari), 98.65 mph; 2nd, A.de Portago/P.J.Collins (Lancia-Ferrari); 3rd, J.Behra (Maserati 250F).

German Grand Prix, Nürburgring (312 miles), 5 August
1st, J.M.Fangio (Lancia-Ferrari), 85.57 mph; 2nd, S.Moss (Maserati 250F); 3rd, J.Behra (Maserati 250F).

European Grand Prix, Monza (311 miles), 2 September
1st, S.Moss (Maserati 250F), 129.75 mph; 2nd, P.J. Collins/J.M.Fangio (Lancia-Ferrari); 3rd, R.Flockhart (Connaught 'Syracuse').

Drivers' World Championship:
1st, J.M.Fangio (30 points); 2nd, S.Moss (27 points); 3rd, P.J.Collins (25 points).

1957:

Argentine Grand Prix, Buenos Aires (three hours), 13 January
1st, J.M.Fangio (Maserati 250F), 80.47 mph; 2nd, J.Behra (Maserati 250F); 3rd, C.Menditeguy (Maserati 250F).

Monaco Grand Prix, Monte Carlo (205 miles), 19 May
1st, J.M.Fangio (Maserati 250F), 64.72 mph; 2nd, C.A.S. Brooks (Vanwall); 3rd, M.Gregory (Maserati 250F).

French Grand Prix, Rouen (313 miles), 7 July
1st, J.M.Fangio (Maserati 250F), 100.02 mph; 2nd, L.Musso (Lancia-Ferrari Tipo 801); 3rd, P.J.Collins (Lancia-Ferrari Tipo 801).

European Grand Prix, Aintree (270 miles), 20 July
1st, C.A.S.Brooks/S.Moss (Vanwall), 86.80 mph; 2nd, L.Musso (Lancia-Ferrari Tipo 801); 3rd, J.M.Hawthorn (Lancia-Ferrari Tipo 801).

German Grand Prix, Nürburgring (312 miles), 4 August
1st, J.M.Fangio (Maserati 250F), 88.82 mph; 2nd, J.M. Hawthorn (Lancia-Ferrari Tipo 801); 3rd, P.J.Collins (Lancia-Ferrari Tipo 801).

Pescara Grand Prix, Pescara (289 miles), 18 August
1st, S.Moss (Vanwall), 95.52 mph; 2nd, J.M.Fangio (Maserati 250F); 3rd, H.Schell (Maserati 250F).

Italian Grand Prix, Monza (311 miles), 8th September
1st, S. Moss (Vanwall), 120.27 mph; 2nd, J. M. Fangio (Maserati 250F); 3rd, W. von Trips (Lancia-Ferrari Tipo 801).

Drivers' World Championship:
1st, J. M. Fangio (40 points); 2nd, S. Moss (25 points); 3rd, L. Musso (16 points).

1958:

Argentine Grand Prix, Buenos Aires (194 miles), 18 January
1st, S. Moss (Cooper-Climax entered by Rob Walker), 83.56 mph; 2nd, L. Musso (Ferrari Dino 246); 3rd, J. M. Hawthorn (Ferrari Dino 246).

Monaco Grand Prix, Monte Carlo (195 miles), 18 May
1st, M. Trintignant (Cooper-Climax entered by Rob Walker), 67.99 mph; 2nd, L. Musso (Ferrari Dino 246); 3rd, P. J. Collins (Ferrari Dino 246).

Dutch Grand Prix, Zandvoort (195 miles), 26 May
1st, S. Moss (Vanwall), 93·95 mph; 2nd, H. Schell (B.R.M.): 3rd, J. Behra (B.R.M.).

European Grand Prix, Spa-Francorchamps (210 miles), 15 June
1st, C. A. S. Brooks (Vanwall), 129.92 mph; 2nd, J. M. Hawthorn (Ferrari Dino 246); 3rd, S. Lewis-Evans (Vanwall).

French Grand Prix, Reims (258 miles), 7 July
1st, J. M. Hawthorn (Ferrari Dino 246), 125.46 mph; 2nd, S. Moss (Vanwall); 3rd, W. von Trips (Ferrari Dino 246).

British Grand Prix Silverstone (220 miles), 20 July
1st, P. J. Collins (Ferrari Dino 246), 102. 05 mph; 2nd, J. M. Hawthorn (Ferrari Dino 246); 3rd, R. Salvadori (Cooper-Climax).

German Grand Prix, Nürburgring (213 miles), 3 August
1st, C. A. S. Brooks (Vanwall), 90.31 mph; 2nd, R. Salvadori (Cooper-Climax); 3rd, M. Trintignant (Cooper-Climax entered by Rob Walker).

Portuguese Grand Prix, Porto (230 miles), 24 August
1st, S. Moss (Vanwall), 105.03 mph; 2nd, J. M. Hawthorn (Ferrari Dino 246); 3rd, S. Lewis-Evans (Vanwall).

Italian Grand Prix, Monza (250 miles), 7 September
1st, C. A. S. Brooks (Vanwall), 121.21 mph; 2nd, J. M. Hawthorn (Ferrari Dino 256); 3rd, P. Hill (Ferrari Dino 246).

Moroccan Grand Prix, Ain-Diab (251 miles), 19 October
1st, S. Moss (Vanwall), 116.22 mph; 2nd, J. M. Hawthorn (Ferrari Dino 256); 3rd, P. Hill (Ferrari Dino 246).

Drivers' World Championship:
1st, J. M. Hawthorn (42 points); 2nd, S. Moss (41 points); 3rd, C. A. S. Brooks (24 points).

Manufacturers' World Championship:
1st, Vanwall (48 points); 2nd, Ferrari (40 points); 3rd, Cooper (31 points).

1959:

Monaco Grand Prix, Monte Carlo (195 miles), 10 May
1st, J. Brabham (Cooper-Climax), 66.71 mph; 2nd, C. A. S. Brooks (Ferrari Dino 246); 3rd, M. Trintignant (Cooper-Climax entered by Rob Walker).

Dutch Grand Prix, Zandvoort (195 miles), 31 May
1st, J. Bonnier (B.R.M.), 93.46 mph; 2nd, J. Brabham (Cooper-Climax); 3rd, M. Gregory (Cooper-Climax).

European Grand Prix, Reims (258 miles), 5 July
1st, C. A. S. Brooks (Ferrari Dino 246), 127.44 mph; 2nd, P. Hill (Ferrari Dino 246); 3rd, J. Brabham (Cooper-Climax).

British Grand Prix, Aintree (225 miles), 18 July
1st, J. Brabham (Cooper-Climax), 89.88 mph; 2nd, S. Moss (B.R.M. entered by the British Racing Partnership); 3rd, B. McLaren (Cooper-Climax).

German Grand Prix, Avus (Aggregate of two heats totalling 310 miles), 2nd August
1st, C. A. S. Brooks (Ferrari Dino 246), 143.35 mph; 2nd, D. Gurney (Ferrari Dino 246); 3rd, P. Hill (Ferrari Dino 256).

Portuguese Grand Prix, Monsanto, Lisbon (209 miles), 23 August
1st, S. Moss (Cooper-Climax entered by Rob Walker), 95.32 mph; 2nd, M. Gregory (Cooper-Climax); 3rd, D. Gurney (Ferrari Dino 246).

Italian Grand Prix, Monza (257 miles), 13 September
1st, S. Moss (Cooper-Climax entered by Rob Walker), 124.38 mph; 2nd, P. Hill (Ferrari Dino 246); 3rd, J. Brabham (Cooper-Climax).

United States Grand Prix, Sebring (218 miles), 12 December
1st, B. McLaren (Cooper-Climax), 98.83 mph; 2nd, M. Trintignant (Cooper-Climax entered by Rob Walker); 3rd, C. A. S. Brooks (Ferrari Dino 246).

Drivers' World Championship:
1st, J. Brabham (31 points); 2nd, C. A. S. Brooks (27 points); 3rd, S. Moss (25½ points).

Manufacturers' World Championship:
1st, Cooper (40 points); 2nd, Ferrari (32 points); 3rd, B.R.M. (19 points).

1960:

Argentine Grand Prix, Buenos Aires (194 miles), 7 February
1st, B. McLaren (Cooper-Climax), 82.77 mph; 2nd, C. Allison (Ferrari Dino 246); 3rd, M. Trintignant/S. Moss (Cooper-Climax entered by Rob Walker).

Monaco Grand Prix, Monte Carlo (195 miles), 29 May
1st, S. Moss (Lotus 18-Climax entered by Rob Walker), 67.46 mph; 2nd, B. McLaren (Cooper-Climax); 3rd, P. Hill (Ferrari Dino 246).

Dutch Grand Prix, Zandvoort (195 miles), 6 June
1st, J. Brabham (Cooper-Climax), 96.27 mph; 2nd, I. Ireland (Lotus-Climax); 3rd, G. Hill (B.R.M.).

Belgian Grand Prix, Spa-Francorchamps (315 miles), 19 June
1st, J. Brabham (Cooper-Climax), 133.62 mph; 2nd, B. McLaren (Cooper-Climax); 3rd, O. Gendebien (Cooper-Climax entered by the Yeoman Credit Team).

French Grand Prix, Reims (258 miles), 3 July
1st, J. Brabham (Cooper-Climax), 132.19 mph; 2nd, O. Gendebien (Cooper-Climax entered by the Yeoman Credit Team); 3rd, B. McLaren (Cooper-Climax).

British Grand Prix, Silverstone (225 miles), 16 July
1st, J. Brabham (Cooper-Climax), 108.69 mph; 2nd, J. Surtees (Lotus 18-Climax); 3rd, I. Ireland (Lotus 18-Climax).

Portuguese Grand Prix, Porto (253 miles), 14 August
1st, J. Brabham (Cooper-Climax), 109.27 mph; 2nd, B. McLaren (Cooper-Climax); 3rd, J. Clark (Lotus 18-Climax).

European Grand Prix, Monza (311 miles), 4 September
1st, P. Hill (Ferrari Dino 246), 132.06 mph; 2nd, R. Ginther (Ferrari Dino 246); 3rd, W. Mairesse (Ferrari Dino 246).

United States Grand Prix, Riverside (246 miles), 20 November
1st, S. Moss (Lotus 18-Climax entered by Rob Walker), 99.00 mph; 2nd, I. Ireland (Lotus 18-Climax); 3rd, B. McLaren (Cooper-Climax).

Drivers' World Championship:
1st, J. Brabham (43 points); 2nd, B. McLaren (34 points); 3rd, S. Moss (19 points).

Manufacturers' World Championship:
1st, Cooper (40 points); 2nd, Lotus (32 points); 3rd, Ferrari (24 points).

1961:

Monaco Grand Prix, Monte Carlo (195 miles), 14 May
1st, S. Moss (Lotus 18-Climax entered by Rob Walker), 70.70 mph; 2nd, R. Ginther (Ferrari Tipo 156); 3rd, P. Hill (Ferrari Tipo 156).

Dutch Grand Prix, Zandvoort (195 miles), 22 May
1st, W. von Trips (Ferrari Tipo 156), 96. 21 mph; 2nd, P. Hill (Ferrari Tipo 156); 3rd, J. Clark (Lotus 21-Climax).

Belgian Grand Prix, Spa-Francorchamps (263 miles), 18 June
1st, P. Hill (Ferrari Tipo 156), 128.15 mph; 2nd, W. von Trips (Ferrari Tipo 156); 3rd, R. Ginther (Ferrari Tipo 156).

French Grand Prix, Reims (268 miles), 2 July
1st, G. Baghetti (Ferrari Tipo 156), 119.84 mph; 2nd, D. Gurney (Porsche); 3rd, J. Clark (Lotus 21-Climax).

British Grand Prix, Aintree (225 miles), 15 July
1st, W. von Trips (Ferrari Tipo 156), 83.91 mph; 2nd, P. Hill (Ferrari Tipo 156); 3rd, R. Ginther (Ferrari Tipo 156).

European Grand Prix, Nürburgring (213 miles), 6 August
1st, S. Moss (Lotus 18-Climax entered by Rob Walker), 92.34 mph; 2nd, W. von Trips (Ferrari Tipo 156); 3rd, P. Hill (Ferrari Tipo 156).

Italian Grand Prix, Monza (267 miles), 10 September
1st, P. Hill (Ferrari Tipo 156), 130.08 mph; 2nd, D. Gurney (Porsche); 3rd, B. McLaren (Cooper-Climax).

United States Grand Prix, Watkins Glen (230 miles), 8 October
1st, I. Ireland (Lotus 21-Climax), 103.17 mph; 2nd, D. Gurney (Porsche); 3rd, C. A. S. Brooks (B.R.M.-Climax).

Drivers' World Championship:
1st, P. Hill (34 points); 2nd, W. von Trips (33 points); 3rd, S. Moss/D. Gurney (21 points).

Manufacturers' World Championship:
1st, Ferrari (40 points); 2nd, Lotus (32 points); 3rd, Porsche (22 points).

1962:

European Grand Prix, Zandvoort (208 miles), 20 May
1st, G. Hill (B.R.M.), 95.44 mph; 2nd T. Taylor (Lotus 24-Climax); 3rd, P. Hill (Ferrari Tipo 156).

Monaco Grand Prix, Monte Carlo (195 miles), 3rd June
1st, B. McLaren (Cooper-Climax), 70.46 mph; 2nd, P. Hill (Ferrari Tipo 156); 3rd, L. Bandini (Ferrari Tipo 156).

Belgian Grand Prix, Spa-Francorchamps (280 miles), 17 June
1st, J. Clark (Lotus 25-Climax), 131.89 mph; 2nd, G. Hill (B.R.M.); 3rd, P. Hill (Ferrari Tipo 156).

French Grand Prix, Rouen (219 miles), 8 July
1st, D. Gurney (Porsche), 101.89 mph; 2nd, A. Maggs (Cooper-Climax); 3rd, R. Ginther (B.R.M.).

British Grand Prix, Aintree (225 miles), 21 July
1st, J. Clark (Lotus 25-Climax), 92.25 mph; 2nd, J. Surtees (Lola-Climax); 3rd, B. McLaren (Cooper-Climax).

German Grand Prix, Nürburgring (213 miles), 5 August
1st, G. Hill (B.R.M.), 80.28 mph; 2nd, J. Surtees (Lola-Climax); 3rd, D. Gurney (Porsche).

Italian Grand Prix, Monza (307 miles), 16th September
1st, G. Hill (B.R.M.), 123.62 mph; 2nd, R. Ginther (B.R.M.); 3rd, B. McLaren (Cooper-Climax).

United States Grand Prix, Watkins Glen (230 miles), 7 October
1st, J. Clark (Lotus 25-Climax), 108.61 mph; 2nd, G. Hill (B.R.M.); 3rd, B. McLaren (Cooper-Climax).

South African Grand Prix, East London (200 miles), 29 December
1st, G. Hill (B.R.M.), 93.57 mph; 2nd, B. McLaren (Cooper-Climax); 3rd, A. Maggs (Cooper-Climax).

Drivers' World Championship:
1st, G. Hill (42 points); 2nd, J. Clark (30 points); 3rd, B. McLaren (27 points).

Manufacturers' World Championship:
1st, B.R.M. (42 points); 2nd, Lotus (36 points); 3rd, Cooper (29 points).

1963:

European Grand Prix, Monte Carlo (195 miles), 26 May
1st, G. Hill (B.R.M.), 72.43 mph; 2nd, R. Ginther (B.R.M.); 3rd, B. McLaren (Cooper-Climax).

Belgian Grand Prix, Spa-Francorchamps (280 miles), 9 June
1st, J. Clark (Lotus 25-Climax), 131.89 mph; 2nd, B. McLaren (Cooper-Climax); 3rd, D. Gurney (Brabham BT7-Climax).

Dutch Grand Prix, Zandvoort (208 miles), 23 June
1st, J. Clark (Lotus 25-Climax), 97.53 mph; 2nd, D. Gurney (Brabham BT7-Climax); 3rd, J. Surtees (Ferrari Tipo 156).

French Grand Prix, Reims (273 miles), 30 June
1st, J. Clark (Lotus 25-Climax), 125.31 mph; 2nd, A. Maggs (Cooper-Climax); 3rd, G. Hill (B.R.M.).

British Grand Prix, Silverstone (240 miles), 20 July
1st, J. Clark (Lotus 25-Climax), 107.75 mph; 2nd, J. Surtees (Ferrari Tipo 156); 3rd, G. Hill (B.R.M.).

German Grand Prix, Nürburgring (213 miles), 4 August
1st, J. Surtees (Ferrari Tipo 156), 95.83 mph; 2nd, J. Clark (Lotus 25-Climax); 3rd, R. Ginther (B.R.M.).

Italian Grand Prix, Monza (307 miles), 8 September
1st, J. Clark (Lotus 25-Climax), 127,74 mph; 2nd, R. Ginther (B.R.M.); 3rd, B. McLaren (Cooper-Climax).

United States Grand Prix, Watkins Glen (253 miles), 6 October
1st, G. Hill (B.R.M.), 108.91 mph; 2nd, R. Ginther (B.R.M.); 3rd, J. Clark (Lotus 25-Climax).

Mexican Grand Prix, Magdalena Mixhuca (202 miles), 27 October
1st, J. Clark (Lotus 25-Climax), 93.30 mph; 2nd, J. Brabham (Brabham BT7-Climax); 3rd, R. Ginther (B.R.M.).

South African Grand Prix, East London (207 miles), 28 December
1st, J. Clark (Lotus 25-Climax), 95.10 mph; 2nd, D. Gurney (Brabham BT7-Climax); 3rd, G. Hill (B.R.M.).

Drivers' World Championship:
1st, J. Clark (54 points); 2nd, G. Hill (29 points); 3rd, R. Ginther (28 points).

Manufacturers' World Championship:
1st, Lotus (54 points); 2nd, B.R.M. (36 points); 3rd, Brabham (28 points).

1964:

Monaco Grand Prix, Monte Carlo (195 miles), 10 May
1st, G. Hill (B.R.M.), 73.04 mph; 2nd, R. Ginther (B.R.M.); 3rd, P. Arundell (Lotus 25C-Climax).

Dutch Grand Prix, Zandvoort (208 miles), 24 May
1st, J. Clark (Lotus 25D-Climax), 98.02 mph; 2nd, J. Surtees (Ferrari Tipo 158); 3rd, P. Arundell (Lotus 25C-Climax).

Belgian Grand Prix, Spa-Francorchamps (280 miles), 14 June
1st, J. Clark (Lotus 25D-Climax), 132.79 mph; 2nd, B. McLaren (Cooper-Climax); 3rd, J. Brabham (Brabham BT11-Climax).

French Grand Prix, Rouen-les-Essarts (233 miles), 28 June
1st, D. Gurney (Brabham BT11-Climax), 108.77 mph; 2nd, G. Hill (B.R.M.); 3rd, J. Brabham (Brabham BT11-Climax).

European Grand Prix, Brands Hatch (212 miles), 11 July
1st, J. Clark (Lotus 33-Climax), 94.14 mph; 2nd, G. Hill (B.R.M.); 3rd, J. Surtees (Ferrari Tipo 158).

German Grand Prix, Nürburgring (213 miles), 2 August
1st, J. Surtees (Ferrari Tipo 158), 96.57 mph; 2nd, G. Hill (B.R.M.); 3rd, L. Bandini (Ferrari Tipo 156).

Australian Grand Prix, Zeltweg (200 miles), 23 August
1st, L. Bandini (Ferrari Tipo 156), 100.20 mph; 2nd, R. Ginther (B.R.M.); 3rd, R. Anderson (Brabham BT11-Climax privately entered).

Italian Grand Prix, Monza (279 miles), 6 September
1st, J. Surtees (Ferrari Tipo 158), 137.77 mph; 2nd, B. McLaren (Cooper-Climax); 3rd, L. Bandini (Ferrari Tipo 158).

United States Grand Prix, Watkins Glen (253 miles), 4 October
1st, G. Hill (B.R.M.), 111.10 mph; 2nd, J. Surtees (Ferrari Tipo 158); 3rd. J. Siffert (Brabham BT11-B.R.M. entered by Rob Walker).

Mexican Grand Prix, Magdalena Mixhuca (202 miles), 25 October
1st, D. Gurney (Brabham BT11-Climax), 93.33 mph; 2nd, J. Surtees (Ferrari Tipo 158); 3rd, L. Bandini (Ferrari Tipo 1512).

Drivers' World Championship:
1st, J. Surtees (40 points); 2nd, G. Hill (39 points); 3rd, J. Clark (32 points).

Manufacturers' World Championship:
1st, Ferrari (45 points); 2nd, B.R.M. (42 points); 3rd, Lotus (38 points).

1965:

South African Grand Prix, East London (207 miles), 1 January
1st, J.Clark (Lotus 33-Climax), 97.97 mph; 2nd, J.Surtees (Ferrari Tipo 158); 3rd, G.Hill (B.R.M.).

Monaco Grand Prix, Monte Carlo (195 miles), 30 May
1st, G.Hill (B.R.M.), 72.43 mph; 2nd, L.Bandini (Ferrari Tipo 1512); 3rd, J.Stewart (B.R.M.).

European Grand Prix, Spa-Francorchamps (280 miles), 13 June
1st, J.Clark (Lotus 33-Climax), 117.16 mph; 2nd, J.Stewart (B.R.M.); 3rd, B.McLaren (Cooper-Climax).

French Grand Prix, Clermont-Ferrand (200 miles), 27 June
1st, J.Clark (Lotus 33-Climax), 89.20 mph; 2nd, J.Stewart (B.R.M.); 3rd, J.Surtees (Ferrari Tipo 158).

British Grand Prix, Silverstone (234 miles), 10 July
1st, J.Clark (Lotus 33-Climax), 112.02 mph; 2nd, G.Hill (B.R.M.); 3rd, J.Surtees (Ferrari Tipo 1512).

Dutch Grand Prix, Zandvoort (221 miles), 18 July
1st, J. Clark (Lotus 33-Climax), 100·87 mph; 2nd, J. Stewart (B.R.M.); 3rd, D. Gurney (Brabham BT11-Climax).

German Grand Prix, Nürburgring (213 miles), 1 August
1st, J.Clark (Lotus 33-Climax), 99.79 mph; 2nd, G.Hill (B.R.M.); 3rd, D.Gurney (Brabham BT11-Climax).

Italian Grand Prix, Monza (272 miles), 12 September
1st, J.Stewart (B.R.M.), 130.46 mph; 2nd, G.Hill (B.R.M.); 3rd, D.Gurney (Brabham BT11-Climax).

United States Grand Prix, Watkins Glen (253 miles), 3 October
1st, G.Hill (B.R.M.), 107.98 mph; 2nd, D.Gurney (Brabham BT11-Climax); 3rd, J.Brabham (Brabham BT11-Climax).

Mexican Grand Prix, Magdalena Mixhuca (202 miles), 24 October
1st, R.Ginther (Honda), 94.26 mph; 2nd, D.Gurney (Brabham BT11-Climax); 3rd, M.Spence (Lotus 33-Climax).

Drivers' World Championship:
1st, J.Clark (54 points); 2nd, G.Hill (40 points); 3rd, J.Stewart (33 points).

Manufacturers' World Championship:
1st, Lotus (54 points); 2nd, B.R.M. (45 points); 3rd, Brabham (27 points).

1966:

Monaco Grand Prix, Monte Carlo (195 miles), 22 May
1st, J.Stewart (B.R.M. 2-litre), 76.52 mph; 2nd, L.Bandini (Ferrari Dino 246); 3rd, G.Hill (B.R.M.).

Belgian Grand Prix, Spa-Francorchamps (245 miles), 12 June
1st, J.Surtees (Ferrari Tipo 312), 113.39 mph; 2nd J.Rindt (Cooper-Maserati); 3rd, L.Bandini (Ferrari Dino 246).

European Grand Prix, Reims (248 miles), 3 July
1st, J.Brabham BT19-Repco), 136.90 mph; 2nd, M.Parkes (Ferrari Tipo 312); 3rd, D.Hulme (Brabham BT20-Repco).

British Grand Prix, Brands Hatch (202 miles), 16 July
1st, J.Brabham (Brabham BT19-Repco), 95.48 mph; 2nd, D. Hulme (Brabham BT20-Repco); 3rd, G.Hill (B.R.M. 2-litre).

Dutch Grand Prix, Zandvoort (234 miles), 24 July
1st, J.Brabham (Brabham BT19-Repco), 100.10 mph; 2nd, G. Hill (B.R.M. 2-litre); 3rd, J. Clark (Lotus 33-Climax 2-litre).

German Grand Prix, Nürburgring (213 miles), 7 August
1st, J.Brabham (Brabham BT19-Repco), 86.75 mph; 2nd, J. Surtees (Cooper-Maserati); 3rd, J. Rindt (Cooper-Maserati).

Italian Grand Prix, Monza (243 miles), 4 September
1st, L.Scarfiotti (Ferrari 312), 135.93 mph; 2nd, M.Parkes (Ferrari Tipo 312); 3rd, D.Hulme (Brabham BT20-Repco).

United States Grand Prix, Watkins Glen (248 miles), 2 October
1st, J.Clark (Lotus 43-B.R.M.), 114.94 mph; 2nd, J.Rindt (Cooper-Maserati); 3rd, J.Surtees (Cooper-Maserati).

Mexican Grand Prix, Magdalena Mixhuca (202 miles), 23 October
1st, J.Surtees (Cooper-Maserati), 95.72 mph; 2nd, J.Brabham (Brabham BT19-Repco); 3rd, D.Hulme (Brabham BT20-Repco).

Drivers' World Championship:
1st, J.Brabham (42 points); 2nd, J.Surtees (28 points); 3rd, J. Rindt (22 points).

Manufacturers' World Championship:
1st, Brabham (42 points); 2nd, Ferrari (31 points); 3rd, Cooper (30 points).

1967:

South African Grand Prix, Kyalami (204 miles), 2 January
1st, P.Rodriquez (Cooper-Maserati), 97.10 mph; 2nd, J.Love (Cooper-Climax privately entered); 3rd, J.Surtees (Honda).

Monaco Grand Prix, Monte Carlo (195 miles), 7 May
1st, D.Hulme (Brabham BT20-Repco), 75.89 mph; 2nd, G.Hill (Lotus 33-B.R.M. 2-litre); 3rd, C.Amon (Ferrari Tipo 312).

Dutch Grand Prix, Zandvoort (234 miles), 4 June
1st, J.Clark (Lotus 49-Cosworth), 104.49 mph; 2nd, J.Brabham (Brabham BT20-Repco); 3rd, D.Hulme (Brabham BT20-Repco).

Belgian Grand Prix, Spa-Francorchamps (245 miles), 18 June
1st, D.Gurney (Eagle-Weslake), 145.74 mph; 2nd, J.Stewart (B.R.M. H-16); 3rd, C.Amon (Ferrari Tipo 312).

French Grand Prix, Bugatti Circuit, Le Mans (224 miles), 2 July
1st, J.Brabham (Brabham BT24-Repco), 98.90 mph; 2nd, D.

Hulme (Brabham BT24-Repco); 3rd, J.Stewart (B.R.M. 2-litre).

British Grand Prix, Silverstone (240 miles), 15 July
1st, J.Clark (Lotus 49-Climax); 117.64 mph; 2nd, D.Hulme (Brabham BT24-Repco); 3rd, C.Amon (Ferrari Tipo 312).

German Grand Prix, Nürburgring (213 miles), 6 August
1st, D.Hulme (Brabham BT24-Repco), 101.47 mph; 2nd, J. Brabham (Brabham BT24-Repco); 3rd, C.Amon (Ferrari Tipo 312).

Canadian Grand Prix, Mosport Park (220 miles), 27 August
1st, J.Brabham (Brabham BT24-Repco), 105.93 mph; 2nd, D.Hulme (Brabham BT24-Repco); 3rd, D.Gurney (Eagle-Weslake).

European Grand Prix, Monza (243 miles), 10 September
1st, J.Surtees (Honda), 140.50 mph; 2nd, J.Brabham (Brabham BT24-Repco); 3rd, J.Clark (Lotus 49-Cosworth).

United States Grand Prix, Watkins Glen (248 miles), 1 October
1st, J.Clark (Lotus 49-Cosworth), 120.95 mph; 2nd, G.Hill (Lotus 49-Cosworth); 3rd, D.Hulme (Brabham BT24-Repco).

Mexican Grand Prix, Magdalena Mixhuca (202 miles), 22 October
1st, J.Clark (Lotus 49-Cosworth), 101.42 mph; 2nd, J.Brabham (Brabham BT24-Repco); 3rd, D.Hulme (Brabham BT24-Repco).

Drivers' World Championship:
1st, D.Hulme (51 points); 2nd, J.Brabham (46 points); 3rd, J.Clark (41 points).

Manufacturers' World Championship:
1st, Brabham (67 points); 2nd, Lotus (44 points); 3rd, Cooper (28 points).

1968:

South African Grand Prix, Kyalami (204 miles), 1 January
1st, J. Clark (Lotus 49-Cosworth), 107.42 mph; 2nd, G.Hill (Lotus 49-Cosworth); 3rd, J.Rindt (Brabham BT24-Repco).

Spanish Grand Prix, Madrid (190 miles), 12 May
1st, G.Hill (Lotus 49-Cosworth), 86.41 mph; 2nd, D.Hulme (McLaren M7A-Cosworth); 3rd, B.Redman (Cooper-B.R.M.).

Monaco Grand Prix, Monte Carlo (156 miles), 26 May
1st, G.Hill (Lotus 49B-Cosworth), 77.82 mph; 2nd, R.Attwood (B.R.M. P126); 3rd, L.Bianchi (Cooper-B.R.M.).

Belgian Grand Prix, Spa-Francorchamps (245 miles), 9 June
1st, B.McLaren (McLaren M7A-Cosworth), 147.14 mph; 2nd, P.Rodriquez (B.R.M. P133); 3rd, J.Ickx (Ferrari Tipo 312).

Dutch Grand Prix, Zandvoort (234 miles), 23 June
1st, J.Stewart (Matra MS10-Cosworth), 84.66 mph; 2nd, J-P. Beltoise (Matra MS11); 3rd, P.Rodriquez (B.R.M. P133).

French Grand Prix, Rouen les Essarts, (244 miles), 7 July
1st, J.Ickx (Ferrari Tipo 312), 100.45 mph; 2nd, J.Surtees (Honda RA301); 3rd, J.Stewart (Matra MS10-Cosworth).

British Grand Prix, Brands Hatch (212 miles), 20 July
1st, J.Siffert (Lotus 49B-Cosworth), 104.83 mph; 2nd, C.Amon (Ferrari Tipo 312); 3rd, J.Ickx (Ferrari Tipo 312).

European Grand Prix, Nürburgring (199 miles), 4 August
1st, J.Stewart (Matra MS10-Cosworth), 86.86 mph; 2nd, G. Hill (Lotus 49B-Cosworth); 3rd, J.Rindt (Brabham BT26-Repco).

Italian Grand Prix, Monza (243 miles), 8 September
1st, D.Hulme (McLaren M7A-Cosworth), 145.41 mph; 2nd, J.Servoz-Gavin (Matra MS10-Cosworth); 3rd, J.Ickx (Ferrari Tipo 312).

Canadian Grand Prix, St Jovite (238 miles), 22 September
1st, D.Hulme (McLaren M7A-Cosworth), 97.25 mph; 2nd, B.McLaren (McLaren M7A-Cosworth); 3rd, P.Rodriquez (B.R.M. P133).

United States Grand Prix, Watkins Glen (248 miles), 6 October
1st, J.Stewart (Matra MS10-Cosworth), 124.89 mph; 2nd, G. Hill (Lotus 49B-Cosworth); 3rd, J.Surtee (Honda RA301).

Mexican Grand Prix, Magdalena Mixhuca (203 miles), 3 November
1st, G.Hill (Lotus 49B-Cosworth), 103.08 mph; 2nd, B. McLaren (McLaren M7A-Cosworth); 3rd, J.Oliver (Lotus 49B-Cosworth).

Drivers' World Championship:
1st, G.Hill (48 points); 2nd, J.Stewart (36 points); 3rd, D. Hulme (33 points).

Manufacturers' World Championship:
1st, Lotus (64 points); 2nd, Matra (47 points); 3rd, McLaren (46 points).

1969:

South African Grand Prix, Kyalami (204 miles), 1 March
1st, J.Stewart (Matra MS10-Cosworth), 110.62 mph; 2nd, G.Hill (Lotus 49B-Cosworth); 3rd, D.Hulme (McLaren M7A-Cosworth).

Spanish Grand Prix, Montjuich Park, Barcelona (212 miles), 4 May
1st, J.Stewart (Matra MS80-Cosworth), 93.89 mph; 2nd, B.McLaren (McLaren M7C-Cosworth); 3rd, J-P.Beltoise (Matra MS80-Cosworth).

Monaco Grand Prix, Monte Carlo (156 miles), 18 May
1st, G.Hill (Lotus 49T/B-Cosworth), 80.18 mph; 2nd, P. Courage (Brabham BT26-Cosworth); 3rd, J.Siffert (Lotus 49B-Cosworth).

Dutch Grand Prix, Zandvoort (235 miles), 21 June
1st, J.Stewart (Matra MS80-Cosworth); 111.04 mph; 2nd, J. Siffert (Lotus 49B-Cosworth); 3rd, C. Amon (Ferrari Tipo 312).

French Grand Prix, Clermont-Ferrand (190 miles), 6 July
1st, J.Stewart (Matra MS80-Cosworth), 97.71 mph; 2nd, J-P. Beltoise (Matra MS80-Cosworth); 3rd, J.Ickx (Brabham BT26-Cosworth).

British Grand Prix, Silverstone (246 miles), 19 July
1st, J.Stewart (Matra MS80-Cosworth), 127.25 mph; 2nd, J.Ickx (Brabham BT26-Cosworth); 3rd, B.McLaren (McLaren M7C-Cosworth).

German Grand Prix, Nürburgring (199 miles), 3 August
1st, J.Ickx (Brabham BT26-Cosworth), 108.43 mph; 2nd, J. Stewart (Matra MS80-Cosworth); 3rd, B.McLaren (McLaren M7C-Cosworth).

Italian Grand Prix, Monza (243 miles), 7 September
1st, J.Stewart (Matra MS80-Cosworth), 146.96 mph; 2nd, J.Rindt (Lotus 49B-Cosworth); 3rd, J-P.Beltoise (Matra MS80-Cosworth).

Canadian Grand Prix, Mosport Park (221 miles), 20 September
1st, J.Ickx (Brabham BT26-Cosworth), 112.76 mph; 2nd, J. Brabham (Brabham BT26-Cosworth); 3rd, J.Rindt (Lotus 49B-Cosworth).

United States Grand Prix, Watkins Glen (248 miles), 5 October
1st, J.Rindt (Lotus 49B-Cosworth), 126.36 mph; 2nd, P. Courage (Brabham BT26-Cosworth); 3rd, J.Surtees (B.R.M. P139).

Mexican Grand Prix, Magdalena Mixhuca (202 miles), 19 October
1st, D.Hulme (McLaren M7A-Cosworth), 106.15 mph; 2nd, J.Ickx (Brabham BT26-Cosworth); 3rd, J.Brabham (Brabham BT26-Cosworth).

Drivers' World Championship:
1st, J.Stewart (63 points); 2nd, J.Ickx (37 points); 3rd, B. McLaren (26 points).

Manufacturers' World Championship:
1st, Matra (66 points); 2nd, Brabham (51 points); 3rd Lotus (44 points).

1970:

South African Grand Prix, Kyalami (204 miles), 7 March
1st, J.Brabham (Brabham BT33-Cosworth), 111.70 mph; 2nd, D.Hulme (McLaren M14A-Cosworth); 3rd, J.Stewart (March 701-Cosworth).

Spanish Grand Prix, Jarama (190 miles), 19 April
1st, J.Stewart (March 701-Cosworth), 87.21 mph; 2nd, B. McLaren (McLaren M14A-Cosworth); 3rd, M.Andretti (March 701-Cosworth).

Monaco Grand Prix, Monte Carlo (156 miles), 10 May
1st, J.Rindt (Lotus 49C-Cosworth), 81.84 mph; 2nd, J.Brabham (Brabham BT33-Cosworth); 3rd, H. Pescarolo (Matra MS120).

Belgian Grand Prix, Spa-Francorchamps (245 miles), 7 June
1st, P.Rodriguez (B.R.M. P153), 149.94 mph; 2nd, C.Amon (March 701-Cosworth); 3rd, J-P.Beltoise (Matra MS120).

Dutch Grand Prix, Zandvoort (209 miles), 21 June
1st, J.Rindt (Lotus 72-Cosworth), 112.95 mph; 2nd, J.Stewart (March 701-Cosworth); 3rd, J.Ickx (Ferrari 312B).

French Grand Prix, Clermont-Ferrand (190 miles), 5 July
1st, J.Rindt (Lotus 72-Cosworth), 98.42 mph; 2nd, C.Amon (March 701-Cosworth); 3rd, J.Brabham (Brabham BT33-Cosworth).

British Grand Prix, Brands Hatch (212 miles), 19 July
1st, J.Rindt (Lotus 72-Cosworth), 108.69 mph; 2nd, J.Brabham (Brabham BT33-Cosworth); 3rd, D.Hulme (McLaren M14D-Cosworth).

German Grand Prix, Hockenheim Motordrom (211 miles), 2 August
1st, J.Rindt (Lotus 72-Cosworth), 123.90 mph; 2nd, J.Ickx (Ferrari 312B); 3rd, D.Hulme (McLaren M14A-Cosworth).

Austrian Grand Prix, Osterreichring (220 miles), 16 August
1st, J.Ickx (Ferrari 312B), 129.27 mph; 2nd, C.Regazzoni (Ferrari 312B); 3rd, R.Stommelen (Brabham BT33-Cosworth).

Italian Grand Prix, Monza (243 miles), 6 September
1st, C.Regazzoni (Ferrari 312B), 147.07 mph; 2nd, J.Stewart (March 701-Cosworth); 3rd, J-P. Beltoise (Matra MS120).

Canadian Grand Prix, St Jovite (238 miles), 20 September
1st, J.Ickx (Ferrari 312B), 101.27 mph; 2nd, C. Regazzoni (Ferrari 312B); 3rd, C.Amon (March 701-Cosworth).

United States Grand Prix, Watkins Glen (248 miles), 4 October
1st, E.Fittipaldi (Lotus 72-Cosworth), 126.79 mph; 2nd, P. Rodriguez (B.R.M. P153); 3rd, R.Wisell (Lotus 72-Cosworth).

Mexican Grand Prix, Ricardo Rodriguez (circuit renamed – 202 miles), 25 October
1st, J.Ickx (Ferrari 312B), 106.78 mph; 2nd, C.Regazzoni (Ferrari 312B); 3rd, D.Hulme (McLaren M14A-Cosworth).

Drivers' World Championship:
1st, J.Rindt (45 points); 2nd, J.Ickx (40 points); 3rd, C. Regazzoni (33 points).

Manufacturers' World Championship:
1st, Lotus (59 points); 2nd, Ferrari (51 points); 3rd, March (48 points).